Today's Police and Sheriff Recruits

Insights from the Newest Members of America's Law Enforcement Community

Laura Werber Castaneda, Greg Ridgeway

 Center on Quality Policing

A RAND INFRASTRUCTURE, SAFETY, AND ENVIRONMENT CENTER

This project was supported by Cooperative Agreement 2007CKWXK005 awarded by the Office of Community Oriented Policing Services, U.S. Department of Justice. The opinions, findings, and conclusions or recommendations contained herein are those of the authors and do not necessarily represent the official position of the U.S. Department of Justice. References to specific companies, products, or services should not be considered an endorsement of the product by the authors or the U.S. Department of Justice. Rather, the references are illustrations to supplement discussion of the issues. This project was conducted under the auspices of the RAND Center on Quality Policing (CQP), part of the Safety and Justice Program within RAND Infrastructure, Safety, and Environment (ISE).

Library of Congress Cataloging-in-Publication Data

Castaneda, Laura Werber.
  Today's police and sheriff recruits : insights from the newest members of America's law enforcement community / Laura Werber Castaneda, Greg Ridgeway.
    p. cm.
  ISBN 978-0-8330-5047-2 (pbk. : alk. paper)
  1. Police—Recruiting—United States. 2. Police recruits—United States. 3. Law enforcement—Vocational guidance—United States. 4. Police—Personnel management—United States. 5. Employee retention—United States. I. Ridgeway, Greg, 1973- II. Title.

  HV7936.R5C37 2010
  363.2'20973—dc22

                                                                    2010031286

The RAND Corporation is a nonprofit institution that helps improve policy and decisionmaking through research and analysis. RAND's publications do not necessarily reflect the opinions of its research clients and sponsors.

RAND® is a registered trademark.

Published 2010 by the RAND Corporation
1776 Main Street, P.O. Box 2138, Santa Monica, CA 90407-2138
1200 South Hayes Street, Arlington, VA 22202-5050
4570 Fifth Avenue, Suite 600, Pittsburgh, PA 15213-2665
RAND URL: http://www.rand.org/
To order RAND documents or to obtain additional information, contact
Distribution Services: Telephone: (310) 451-7002;
Fax: (310) 451-6915; Email: order@rand.org

Preface

The Office of Community Oriented Policing Services (COPS) in the U.S. Department of Justice asked RAND to conduct a survey of recent police officer and sheriff's deputy recruits to aid the law enforcement community in refining its recruitment practices and improving recruitment results. The request was motivated in part by the hiring challenges the law enforcement community, particular large municipal agencies, faced in 2007 and in part by the desire to develop a larger workforce well suited to community-oriented policing. Although, as of summer 2010, a financial crisis was affecting most departments' capacity to recruit, all the trends suggest that the next decade will be as challenging as the past decade for recruiting the next generation of police officers.

RAND's survey, fielded from September 2008 through March 2009, targeted new law enforcement recruits themselves, reaching a national pool of respondents representing 44 of the United States' largest police and sheriff's departments. The survey asked recruits about their reasons for pursuing a career in law enforcement, potential disadvantages of such a career, influencers on a career in law enforcement and employment within the recruit's chosen agency, and the perceived effectiveness of both actual and potential recruiting strategies. This report provides the results of the survey, including both findings about the overall survey sample as well as those focused on groups often of particular interest to law enforcement recruitment professionals: women, racial/ethnic minorities, older recruits, recruits from immigrant families, college graduates, recruits with military experience, and recruits with prior law enforcement experience. Recommendations informed by the survey results are also featured in the report.

This report should be of interest to local police agencies faced with the prospect of a shortfall in their recruiting efforts. Other recent and related RAND works that may be of interest to readers of this report include the following:

- Police Recruiting and Retention Clearinghouse, http://cqp.rand.org
- *Police Recruitment and Retention in the Contemporary Urban Environment: A National Discussion of Personnel Experiences and Promising Practices from the Front Lines* (Wilson and Grammich, 2009)
- *To Protect and to Serve: Enhancing the Efficiency of LAPD Recruiting* (Lim et al., 2009)
- *Strategies for Improving Officer Recruitment in the San Diego Police Department* (Ridgeway et al., 2008)
- *Recruitment and Retention: Lessons for the New Orleans Police Department* (Rostker, Hix, and Wilson, 2007).

The RAND Center on Quality Policing

This research was conducted under the auspices of the RAND Center on Quality Policing within the Safety and Justice Program of RAND Infrastructure, Safety, and Environment (ISE). The Center conducts research and analysis to improve contemporary police practice and policy. The mission of ISE is to improve the development, operation, use, and protection of society's essential physical assets and natural resources and to enhance the related social assets of safety and security of individuals in transit and in their workplaces and communities. Safety and Justice Program research addresses occupational safety, transportation safety, food safety, and public safety—including violence, policing, corrections, substance abuse, and public integrity.

Questions or comments about this monograph should be sent to the lead author, Laura Castaneda (Laura_Castaneda@rand.org). Information about the Safety and Justice Program is available online (http://www.rand.org/ise/safety), as is information about the Center on Quality Policing (http://cqp.rand.org). Inquiries about research projects should be sent to the following address:

Greg Ridgeway, Director
Safety and Justice Program
RAND Corporation
1776 Main St.
Santa Monica, CA 90407-2138
310-393-0411 x7734
sjdirector@rand.org

Contents

Figures

Tables

Summary

Introduction

The Office of Community Oriented Policing Services in the U.S. Department of Justice asked RAND to conduct a survey of recent police officer and sheriff's deputy recruits to aid the law enforcement community in refining its recruitment practices and improving recruitment results. The request was motivated in part by the hiring challenges the law enforcement community, particular large municipal agencies, faced in 2007 and in part by the desire to develop a larger workforce well suited to community-oriented policing. RAND's survey, fielded from September 2008 through March 2009, targeted new law enforcement recruits themselves, reaching a national pool of respondents representing 44 of the United States' largest police and sheriff's departments.

Survey questions pertain to recruits' reasons for pursuing a career in law enforcement, potential disadvantages of such a career, influencers on a career in law enforcement and employment within the recruit's chosen agency, and the perceived effectiveness of both actual and potential recruiting strategies. The survey benefited from a high overall response rate (80 percent), and the 1,619 survey respondents included a notable proportion of women (16 percent) and racial/ethnic minorities (45 percent). Moreover, the survey sample was large enough to extract some information from small subpopulations, such as Asian recruits (3 percent). This report provides the results of the survey, including both findings about the overall survey sample as well as those focused on groups often of particular interest to law enforcement recruitment professionals: women, racial/ethnic minorities, older recruits, recruits from immigrant families, college graduates, recruits with military experience, and recruits with prior law enforcement experience. Some departments have developed strategies to increase their workforce diversity, specifically by hiring more women and racial/ethnic minorities, as part of efforts to improve police-community relations and more effectively implement community-oriented policing. Recommendations informed by the survey results are also featured in the report.

Pros and Cons of Law Enforcement Careers

When asked to indicate their primary reasons for entering law enforcement, recruits gave the greatest emphasis to job security and helping the community. After such background characteristics as age, gender, and education were taken into account, older recruits (age 26 or older) tended to focus on job security more than younger recruits did. In addition, Hispanic recruits and those with prior law enforcement experience gave greater weight to public service aspects of law enforcement. Compared with white recruits, black recruits were more attracted to the prestige of the profession.

Turning our attention to the negative aspects of working in law enforcement, new recruits most frequently identified the threat of death or injury and insufficient salary as drawbacks of working in law enforcement that were salient during their decision process. Women cited some potential barriers that law enforcement careers may pose for women in particular. Women were more likely to cite fitness requirements and family obligations as barriers to joining law enforcement, and they generally rated the public service aspects of the job as more important than they did salary. However, a large majority (nearly 80 percent) of black women rated salary as more important than they did the public service aspects of the job. Overall, black recruits were considerably less likely than white recruits to cite insufficient salary as a key disadvantage. On the other hand, college graduates were much more likely than recruits with less education to report that inadequate pay was a concern during their decision process.

In the survey, recruits were also asked to think of a family member or friend close to them in age and consider why he or she opted not to pursue a career in law enforcement. The characteristics of working in law enforcement that recruits believed dissuaded their peers were somewhat different from the downsides they themselves considered. While similar numbers of recruits noted that insufficient salary factored into their own decisions as well as their peers', when it came to their peers, recruits were inclined to report that their peers' perceptions about the threat of death or injury inherent to law enforcement, competing career interests, long hours, lack of physical fitness, and personal negative views about the police were key barriers to their pursuit of a law enforcement career. Women tended to report that their similarly aged peers were deterred from entering law enforcement by its fitness requirements and perceived difficulties they would encounter meeting family obligations. Black recruits were the least likely of any racial/ethnic group to believe that fitness requirements would be a barrier for their similarly aged peers. Asian recruits, on the other hand, tended to note that their friends and family members found other career options more appealing, suggesting that this is a barrier for departments to overcome when trying to increase Asian representation.

Influences on Recruits' Career Decisions

Given the significant role that an individual's family, friends, and other acquaintances can play in influencing his or her choice of occupation, we provided recruits with a list of potential influencers on their decision process and asked them to indicate whether each individual provided an opinion about their decision to pursue a law enforcement career. Recruits were also instructed to note whether the potential influencer is or was involved in law enforcement and how favorable the opinion offered was. We found that mothers and fathers are key influencers on this decision, with about 80 percent of survey respondents reporting that parents weighed in on their career choice. The majority of recruits also reported that siblings and friends close in age offered opinions. Generally, potential influencers offered neutral to supportive views. Mothers tended to be less supportive than fathers overall, and the nature of their opinion varied more. In addition, half of new recruits received input from law enforcement professionals, and those law enforcement professionals gave the most support for their law enforcement career choice.

Another area of influence we explored in the survey was the factors that influenced recruits to accept employment at the agency that had sent them to training. Job benefits, namely health insurance and retirement plans, were prominent in recruits' decision to work at a specific agency. In particular, Hispanic recruits and older recruits viewed retirement plans as more important than did white recruits and younger recruits, respectively. The agency's reputation and variety in assignments also were widely regarded as important decision factors. Although not highly rated by the overall sample, affordability of housing emerged as a consideration for black recruits, Hispanic recruits, and those from immigrant families.

Recruiting Strategies

The survey also provided insights regarding recruiting strategies that law enforcement agencies use or could use to attract new officers and deputies. When asked to indicate what first prompted them to consider working in their current law enforcement agency, recruits most often cited friends and relatives in law enforcement, particularly those already working in the same agency. Among the formal advertising outlets agencies typically used (e.g., television, billboard, newspaper, career fair), the Internet was by far the most popular among the recruits surveyed: 18 percent of respondents identified it as an information source that initially motivated them to contact their current employer.

In addition, recruits also evaluated potential actions and incentives that might improve recruiting for their law enforcement agency. Such financial incentives as a better pension, higher starting salary, support for the purchase of uniforms and other supplies, and a signing bonus were viewed as most effective by the overall survey sample. However, other strategies tended to be important to particular groups of recruits. For example, female recruits, Hispanic recruits, younger recruits, and those with prior law enforcement experience viewed free training and exercise programs to help meet physical standards as more effective than did other recruits. Likewise, college graduates, recruits with military experience, and those with prior law enforcement experience rated choice in job duties or assignments more highly. These results suggest that law enforcement agencies may have options other than financial incentives at their disposal to attract recruits.

Recommendations

The responses from this national sample of new police officer and sheriff's deputy recruits suggest some recommendations for departments developing recruiting strategies.

1. *Target the perceptions of would-be recruits and their potential influencers.* Agencies should emphasize the positive aspects of law enforcement and address negative perceptions, particularly those based on inaccurate information. Respondents noted that their peers likely avoided law enforcement because of a fear of death. The reality is that, in recent years, police officers have had lower fatality rates than farmers, truck and taxi drivers, construction workers, and bartenders. While policing is more dangerous than the average job, the safety record of modern policing deserves greater recognition.

2. *Recognize the value of both financial and nonfinancial motivators.* This survey corroborates past research in noting that many recruits are drawn to law enforcement for nonpecuniary reasons. We also found that the recruits surveyed did not seem dissatisfied with the salary and benefits offered by the agency with which they accepted employment. These findings suggest both that law enforcement agencies should not assume that salary is an insurmountable recruiting obstacle and that greater emphasis on the nonfinancial benefits of law enforcement is warranted.

3. *Fully engage current officers and staff in agency recruiting efforts.* Friends or family working at the department that the recruits ultimately joined were responsible for first prompting more than 40 percent of new recruits to consider the agency. An additional 20 percent were prompted by friends and family at another agency. Further, half of the new recruits surveyed sought out the advice of law enforcement members when they were considering their career choices. These findings suggest that those expressly tasked with recruiting should not be the only agency employees working to attract promising candidates. On the contrary, a department's current officers and civilian staff can be its most effective recruiters.

4. *Expand the agency's Internet presence.* When asked what first motivated them to contact their current employer, 18 percent of recruits surveyed cited an Internet advertisement. In addition, 80 percent of respondents reported accessing the Internet at least daily. Relatively low-cost or even free vehicles for increasing an agency's Internet presence are available, including job sites such as Monster.com and social networking ones such as Facebook, potentially enabling agencies to employ several of them. Such a multipronged Internet strategy may help make a specific law enforcement agency salient in the minds of prospective candidates.

5. *Develop strategies to recruit a workforce well suited to community-oriented policing.* Should law enforcement departments perceive a need to target certain types of recruits given attrition, workforce growth, or a shift in hiring priorities, the results of our survey provide the means to do so. Specifically, law enforcement agencies can appeal to what different types of recruit view as advantages or benefits of working in law enforcement in conjunction with addressing what they perceive to be downsides of a law enforcement career.

6. *Continue to learn from new recruits.* This study demonstrates the value in surveying not only law enforcement executives, as past efforts have done, but also the newest additions to police and sheriff's departments. The results of this survey can serve

not only as a source of ideas of recruiting strategies but also as a benchmark against which agencies may compare themselves over time.

Acknowledgments

This project was supported by Cooperative Agreement Number 2007CKWXK005 awarded by the Office of Community Oriented Policing Services.

We would like to thank several people for their work on project and their contributions toward its success. RAND researchers Carl Matthies and Keith Gierlack spent a substantial amount of time interacting with academy directors and police recruiting operations to engage them in the survey. The high response rates we obtained are largely due to their persuasiveness and persistence with the departments. Amanda Cross, a RAND criminologist, and Michael White, professor of criminal justice at Arizona State University, reviewed this report. We greatly appreciated their constructive comments, which we believe have resulted in a clearer and more useful report.

Most importantly, we would like to thank the 44 police and sheriff's departments that made the effort to distribute the survey and, in many cases, made time at their academies to have their newest recruits complete the survey. We also greatly appreciate the willingness of the recruits themselves to participate in the survey, and we value their thoughtful responses.

Abbreviations

COPS   Office of Community Oriented Policing Services
LE   law enforcement
LEMAS Law Enforcement Management and Administrative Statistics
NYPD   New York City Police Department
POST   Peace Officer Standards and Training

CHAPTER ONE

Introduction

Background

In 2007, the Office of Community Oriented Policing Services (COPS) in the U.S. Department of Justice asked RAND's Center on Quality Policing to, among other activities, conduct a survey of recent police officer and sheriff's deputy recruits nationwide in order to help the law enforcement community improve its recruitment practices and results.

While other research has surveyed departments about their recruiting practices (e.g. Taylor et al., 2005), recent efforts have not targeted new recruits. Further, although why certain people choose law enforcement careers has been of interest for decades, to our knowledge there has never been a national survey of law enforcement recruits conducted for this purpose. In their review, Raganella and White (2004) traced research on the motivations for entering law enforcement back to the 1950s. The research they cite assessed the relative importance of pecuniary and nonpecuniary reasons as well as differences in motivations by gender and race/ethnicity. Other research focuses on whom recruits view as sources of information (e.g., Slater and Reiser, 1988) and work/family conflict (e.g., Ryan et al., 2001). Yet the bulk of these studies are based on surveys of recruits from a particular department. As a consequence, we have learned about motivations in Washington State (Hageman, 1979), influencers in Los Angeles (Slater and Reiser, 1988), and differences between male and female recruits in the Midwest (Meagher and Yentes, 1986), but we know little about how applicable these insights are to recruits at other law enforcement agencies around the country.

Recognizing this gap, as well as the opportunity to build on the decades of agency-specific knowledge, we conducted a survey aimed at obtaining a national view of police recruits regarding why they chose law enforcement, as well as less frequently studied topics (e.g., disadvantages of working in law enforcement). Accordingly, RAND's survey was designed to elicit answers to the following questions: Why pursue a career in law enforcement? Why this agency? What are the downsides of a law enforcement career? What could be done to improve your department's recruiting efforts?

While the focus of the research in this report is on understanding the new recruit so as to develop better recruiting strategies, a department can grow only if recruiting gains are not offset by turnover. It is possible that a better understanding of recruits and their motivations could help agencies target new hires that have a better understanding of the job and consequently are less likely to leave their hiring agency.

We started this project in an extremely tight labor market. For example, in 2007, the San Diego Police Department was understaffed by more than 10 percent, 208 fewer than authorized (Ridgeway et al., 2008), and by mid-2008 the Chicago Police Department was down by the same percentage, with 1,400 officers fewer than authorized (Dardick and Rozas, 2008). The RAND Center on Quality Policing conducted a workshop in 2008, with several major police departments in attendance, aimed at sharing lessons learned on police recruiting (Wilson and Grammich, 2009). The workshop was replete with stories of the intense recruiting efforts necessary even to maintain department sizes; for instance, the Las Vegas Metro Police Department reported needing to hire 400 new officers annually, and Arlington County, Virginia, has a 10 percent turnover rate each year, largely driven by officers leaving for federal law enforcement jobs. Despite such hiring efforts, through 2007 and into 2008 departments struggled to maintain their size.

By the end of 2008, the effects of the financial crisis were finding their way to police and sheriff recruiting. Police departments soon had large numbers of applicants sitting to take written tests. Since the crisis had not quite hit city budgets, or cities had not quite recognized the problems looming, police departments that had struggled earlier in the year to maintain their size or meet their authorized strength were now making their monthly targets. At a Seattle Police Department test in September 2008, the room was filled to capacity, with 112 applicants sitting for the test, four times more than appeared for the January 2008 test (Castro, 2009). This roughly corresponds with the period during which we surveyed new police and sheriff's deputy recruits. At the time of this writing, in summer 2010, local budgets in many communities have tightened, forcing departments to limit new hires or even cut sworn staff. In Los Angeles, after hiring nearly 1,000 new officers in recent years, the city has begun debating layoffs in addition to furloughs to fill a budget gap (Reston and Willon, 2010). In late December 2009, the City of Cleveland sent layoff notices to 67 police officers (Guillen, 2009), which went into effect in early January 2010.

Because states and cities have balanced-budget requirements, police hiring tends to be procyclical, meaning that it occurs when the economy is strong and cities have strong revenues, which tends to be associated with low unemployment rates. As a result departments essentially purchase new labor when hiring is expensive. In contrast, countercyclical spending, something the federal government engages in to stimulate in economic downturns, would result in a less expensive acquisition of new labor but would generally break balanced-budget ordinances.

Consequently, recruiting challenges are likely to return soon enough. Since standard police pension plans give officers retirement benefits after 20 years of service, this helps to create 20-year cycles in police hiring and retirement. Police recruiting was light in the late 1980s, which partly accounts for the lack of mass retirements in the late 2000s. Unemployment rates in 2010 also provide a large disincentive to leave a law enforcement career, implying that employees who would, under normal conditions, change careers are instead accumulating within departments and could separate in short order when the economy recovers. Furthermore, the mid-1990s witnessed an increase in police officers nationally. Between 1996 and 2000, police departments increased by 5 percent, and sheriff's departments increased by 10 percent (Reaves and Hickman, 2004). This increase was partly stimulated by the creation of the COPS office in 1994, which promoted community-oriented policing by putting 100,000 new officers on the street in the 1990s, a 15 percent increase. This suggests that police departments may expect this cohort to retire between 2014 and 2019. Unless communities are willing to tolerate shrinking departments, intense police recruiting will have to begin anew. With the unemployment rate (as of July 2010) nearing 11 percent nationally, and already much higher in some communities, it is a buyer's market for new law enforcement recruits in cities that can afford them. But assuming that the economy recovers by 2014, police and sheriff's departments should expect that the experiences of the tight labor market of the early and mid-2000s will return. Departments that are positioned to attract new recruits will be able to avoid the expensive recruiting programs that became necessary during the 2000s (e.g., $10,000 signing bonuses, bounties, applicant mentoring programs, highly polished websites, public relations firms).

Part of that positioning will necessarily involve departments knowing who is the modern recruit at police and sheriff's departments. The results of this survey of new law enforcement recruits are intended to assist police and sheriff's departments in understanding recruits and planning their recruiting strategies for the coming decade.

Approach and Data

Survey Instrument

Since research that directly examines the perceptions of police officer and sheriff's deputy recruits is limited, we opted to focus expressly on recruits themselves rather than on individuals still considering a career in law enforcement or the recruiting professionals tasked with hiring them. We believed this emphasis would provide new insights regarding recruits' motivations, key influences, and opinions about law enforcement that in turn would inform the development of effective recruiting strategies. Accordingly, our survey instrument included questions that covered the following topics:

- personal demographics, including gender, race/ethnicity, immigrant status, education, military experience, and law enforcement experience
- reasons for pursuing a career in law enforcement
- potential influences on choosing a career in law enforcement and employment with the recruit's chosen agency
- perceived disadvantages of working in law enforcement
- suggestions to improve recruiting at the recruit's chosen agency
- nonwork activities, including volunteer work, extracurricular pursuits, and Internet usage.

The actual survey instrument is provided in Appendix A. During its development, we took into consideration previous work on law enforcement recruiting. For example, we revised and incorporated some of the survey items first used by Lester (1983) in his study of state police recruits and later employed by Raganella and White (2004) in their survey of New York City police recruits to identify recruits' primary reasons for entering law enforcement. The instrument used by the California Commission on Peace Officer Standards and Training (POST) to survey recruits at 15 California training academies also informed item development, and the commission's 2006 report underscored the importance of such topics as potential influencers. Scrivner's 2006 study on police recruitment and hiring corroborated the value of understanding recruits' potential influencers and indicated other potentially fruitful lines of inquiry. For example, she reported how one department had a strong interest in hiring individuals with a history of community and volunteer service because that was regarded as a potentially helpful trait for community-oriented policing. She also documented the results of focus groups conducted to understand better the perspective of female and minority law enforcement employees, such as women's concerns about the physical barriers presented by law enforcement and negative public images of police officers that both women and minorities viewed as an impediment. Last, the survey benefited from a pilot test conducted with new recruits at a Los Angeles–area training academy.

Agency Sample and Recruitment

Equipped with this survey, we aimed to reach a random sample of new police officer and sheriff's deputy recruits drawn from major law enforcement agencies across the country. We did not include federal, state, or highway patrol agencies. Initially, we wanted to have all new recruits nationwide to be eligible for the survey, but this proved to be an inefficient approach. Major urban areas face the greatest challenges to recruiting a sufficient number of officers. While most departments, nearly 95 percent, are small (i.e., fewer than 100 officers) and 40 percent of officers work for departments of this size, Taylor and his colleagues (2005) found that agencies with more than 500 officers are the ones that have experienced significant problems attracting an adequate number of qualified applicants. Furthermore, reaching all new recruits would entail contacting potentially hundreds of police and sheriff's departments. Given the project's goals and resources, we focused on the nation's largest police and sheriff's departments, which we defined as having more than 800 sworn staff. As a result of our focus on large departments, our findings may have limited implications for recruiting in smaller departments.[1] Based on data from the National Public Safety Information Bureau (2008), at the time of our research there were 91 agencies that met this criterion. Each of these agencies serves between 200,000 and 10,000,000 residents.

Rather than ask all 91 agencies to participate, we opted to randomly sample 50 of these agencies. We created a randomly sorted list of the 91 agencies and sequentially worked down the list to enroll agencies in the survey. For each department, we made contact with the individual in charge of recruiting or the academy director. To promote participation, we offered to provide a customized report to each agency that returned a sufficient number of surveys (ideally 50 percent of recruits or greater, but a minimum of surveys from 10 respondents to protect their confidentiality). Between May 2008 and August 2008, we contacted 67 agencies, 16 of which did not participate, most frequently

---

[1]   To develop universally relevant recruitment strategies, future research efforts could examine whether and how the challenges of recruiting and the motivations of officers in small departments resemble those of their colleagues at large law enforcement agencies.

because they did not have an academy during the study period or did not have the staff or capacity to manage the survey distribution. One department indicated that it had no problems recruiting and, therefore, did not see a need to participate.

We worked with each of the 51 departments to distribute surveys to their recruits. For some departments, surveys were distributed to new recruits from multiple academy classes during our study timeframe, while for one agency with several simultaneous cohorts, surveys were administered to one cohort—a group of recruits larger than the full recruiting class for other agencies in our study. Typically, all members of one academy class received surveys. In all cases, given our desire to obtain impressions from new recruits at the very start of their law enforcement careers, we made arrangements to survey recruits either soon after they were hired or early in their academy training. Recruits participated in the study between September 2008 and March 2009 and returned the completed surveys to Abt SRBI, which entered the responses and verified the data. Seven of the departments that agreed to participate returned few or no surveys and consequently were not included in our analysis.

The final sample contained data on 1,619 new police and sheriff recruits from 44 departments. As promised, we provided each of these departments with a customized summary of survey responses for its own recruits along with information showing how its recruits compared with the overall survey sample. The overall response rate was 80 percent, based on the number of surveys distributed. Response rates ranged from 27 percent to 100 percent, with 17 departments having a 100 percent response rate. Of these departments represented in the sample, eight were sheriff's departments. Table 1.1 shows that regional representation of the sample of departments closely resembles the regional distribution of the 91 departments with more than 800 sworn staff.

Survey Analysis

Before conducting any analysis, we weighted the survey responses so that the weighted number of responses from each department would be proportional to the total number of recruits the department had

Table 1.1
Comparison of Agency Features, Sample, and Population

Feature	Sampled Agencies (N=44)	Large Agencies (N=91)
Region		
Northeast	9%	14%
Midwest	11%	14%
Southeast	32%	29%
South	23%	18%
West	25%	25%
Number of authorized sworn officers (median)	2,059	1,831
Number of actual sworn officers (median)	1,984	1,739
Number of separations (median)	67	65
Operating budget (median)	$140M	$122M
Has collective bargaining	73%	70%

SOURCE: U.S. Department of Justice, Bureau of Justice Statistics, Law Enforcement Management and Administrative Statistics (LEMAS), 2006.

in 2008. This makes the survey responses a nationally representative sample of new recruits at large departments. After weighting the data, we calculated descriptive statistics for each of the survey items. These statistics are provided in full in Appendix B.

As we moved forward with our analysis, we opted not only to examine the responses of the entire sample of 1,619 respondents but also to consider the responses of the following groups:

- women
- minorities (Asian, black, and Hispanic)
- older recruits (age 26 and up)
- recruits from immigrant families (those who are immigrants themselves or first-generation Americans)
- recruits with a bachelor's degree
- recruits with prior law enforcement experience
- recruits with prior military experience.

We focused on these distinct groups because they are of special interest to large law enforcement agencies. As Taylor and his colleagues (2005) found in their nationwide survey of law enforcement agencies, individuals with prior law enforcement experience were the most frequently targeted group for recruiting, followed by college graduates, racial/ethnic minorities, and women. Departments have long been determined to increase the number of women and minorities in their officer ranks, not only to mirror better the diverse population they serve (California Commission on POST, 2006; Scrivner, 2006) but also because they may exhibit characteristics desirable for community-oriented policing, which stresses problem solving and effective communication (Taylor et al., 2005). Lonsway and her colleagues (2003), for example, noted than women were more likely to implement community-oriented policing and they tended to employ a policing style that relies less on the use of force and more on communication. Similarly, having recent immigrants on the force has been viewed as a means to improve interactions within multicultural communities (Scrivner, 2006). In addition, in her presentation at the RAND Center on Quality Policing's 2008 Recruitment and Hiring Summit, Scrivner noted that complex cognitive skills are among the new skill sets needed by law enforcement agencies and that the new generation of police candidates includes those who are better educated and more like knowledge workers (Wilson and Grammich, 2009). This suggests that an emphasis on recruiting college graduates, regardless of their major, may be warranted.

Note that we intentionally do not address to what degree departments should actively pursue hiring goals based on diversity. In some communities, it is of questionable legality. However, regardless of a department's intent to diversify its force through targeted recruiting, these results will help departments appreciate gender, racial/ethnic, and other demographic differences among their recruits.

Table 1.2 provides descriptive statistics of the sample. Table B.1 in Appendix B gives a more complete description for each of the key groups noted above. In Table 1.2, the first column of numbers pertains to the survey sample. For example, 16 percent of survey respondents were women, 45 percent of them were racial/ethnic minorities, and

Table 1.2
Survey Sample Demographics: Sex, Race/Ethnicity, Age, Family Status, Education, and Law Enforcement and Military Experience

Characteristic	Survey Sample (%)	All Sworn Officers (%)
Female	16	16
Race/Ethnicity		
Asian	3	2
Black	14	18
Hispanic	25	14
White	56	64
Other	3	1
Age (average 27.3)		
26 and older	58	
Family immigration history		
Recruit is an immigrant	14	
Both parents are immigrants	12	
One parent is an immigrant	8	
One or more grandparents are immigrants	19	
All born in United States	45	
Do not know	2	
Education		
High school graduate, or equivalent	11	
Some college	47	
Bachelor's degree	38	
Advanced degree	3	
Prior law enforcement experience		
This agency	5	
Local government	7	
State government	1	
Federal government	1	

Table 1.2—Continued

Characteristic	Survey Sample (%)	All Sworn Officers (%)
Military police	4	
Private	5	
Other	2	
None	76	
Military service		
Active duty in the past 12 months	7	
Active duty more than 12 months ago	12	
Reserve or National Guard training only	2	
Currently in Reserve or National Guard	6	
Never served in military	79	

SOURCES: 2008–2009 RAND Law Enforcement Recruit Survey, LEMAS data from U.S. Department of Justice, Bureau of Justice Statistics, 2006.

58 percent of them were at least 26 years old. The second column of numbers, from the 2006 Law Enforcement Management and Administrative Statistics (LEMAS), shows how the survey sample compares with all sworn officers in United States in terms of gender and race/ethnicity. Specifically, the gender composition of the survey sample closely resembles the national population captured in LEMAS statistics, and it has a greater proportion of minorities than does the national population.

The remainder of our analysis centered on understanding recruits' perceptions of the pros and cons of law enforcement and identifying influencers on recruits' career decisions. We also asked the recruits to envision barriers that their non–law enforcement peers would cite about why they did not pursue a law enforcement career, giving us a partial view of a potentially greater candidate pool. Although these responses reflect an imperfect measure of the opinions of the recruits' peers, they do provide a window into a group of people that are otherwise difficult to contact and survey.

First, we calculated response frequencies for survey items related to the overarching topics: pros and cons of law enforcement, key influencers, and potential recruiting strategies. Second, we used statistical procedures to determine meaningful patterns present for the groups of interest noted above. More precisely, we first examined unadjusted (i.e., actual) survey responses for statistically significant differences across key groups listed previously: women, minorities, older recruits, immigration history, education, and prior law enforcement and military experience. Next, we used regression models that adjusted for demographic differences to consider how survey responses varied across those same groups of recruits.[2] For each question we flag those groups that answer significantly differently from the other groups. While we have data on other recruit factors that potentially influence their responses, such as marital status and number of dependents, we opted not to include such variables and instead to focus the analysis on factors that departments have previously indicated are of genuine interest.

Last, we reviewed the responses submitted to an open-ended question at the end of survey. When a statistical finding was corroborated by a new recruit's comments, we included those comments to put the finding in the words of the new recruit.

Organization of This Document

Chapter Two covers recruits' perceptions of the pros and cons of law enforcement careers. Chapter Three describes the people that had influence over the new recruits' career decisions and also addresses the aspects of the department that attracted the new recruits. Chapter Four examines strategies currently used by agencies to attract candidates ini-

---

[2]   Throughout the report, we conduct 90 regression models, each with 9 predictor variables. In the process we conduct $90 \times 9 = 810$ statistical tests to identify important predictors of survey responses. We report 180 statistically significant findings at the 0.05 level, a commonly employed statistical threshold. Since there is uncertainty about the magnitude of these effects, testing at the 0.05 level implies that we expect 9 of those 180 findings (5 percent of them) to be due to chance alone. We view this as an acceptable level given the number of questions this report covers.

tially along with recruits' suggestions on how to improve the recruiting process. Chapter Five looks more closely at the survey responses for women and minorities. Finally, Chapter Six provides concluding comments and recommendations for departments to consider in their recruiting efforts.

CHAPTER TWO

Perceived Pros and Cons of Law Enforcement Careers

In this chapter, we summarize police officer and sheriff's deputy recruits' reasons for pursuing a career in law enforcement. We also discuss what they and their peers viewed as potential downsides of a law enforcement career when they were making their career decision. Understanding these views is important to law enforcement recruiting, because appealing to these motivations for entering law enforcement and addressing perceived disadvantages are two general strategies that law enforcement recruiting personnel can employ to attract new recruits more effectively.

Reasons for Pursuing a Law Enforcement Career

We asked new recruits why they wanted to become law enforcement officers. Specifically, we provided them with a list of possible reasons informed by past research (e.g., Lester, 1983; Raganella and White, 2004; California Commission on POST, 2006) and asked them to use a five-point scale to rate how important each was as the time of their decision. Options ranged from "unimportant" to "very important." Figure 2.1 summarizes the responses from the entire survey sample of 1,619 recruits. The tick marks indicate the average response for each reason, and the lines give the range for 80 percent of each reason. For example, the top line shows that 80 percent of the new recruits indicated that job security was a "somewhat important" to "very important" reason for pursuing a career in law enforcement.

Figure 2.1
Reasons That Recruits Gave for Pursuing a Career in Law Enforcement

SOURCE: 2008–2009 RAND Law Enforcement Recruit Survey.
NOTE: The tick marks indicate the average response, and the lines represent the
range for 80 percent of the responses.
RAND *MG992-2.1*

Figure 2.1 indicates that job security and public service (i.e., helping people in the community) were the top two reasons recruits reported for pursuing law enforcement careers. This corroborates past research, typically based on smaller or nonrandom samples, about why people choose to enter law enforcement. Job security was a highly regarded or often cited primary reason in early research on police recruiting: Lester (1983) found that it was an important reason in his survey of state police recruits, and it was the second-ranked reason in Raganella and White's (2004) work with a New York City Police Department (NYPD) recruiting class. Similarly, studies have demonstrated that helping people in the community is a strong motivation for pursuing a career in law enforcement, possibly an even more powerful one than job security: Helping people in the community was the most important reason in Lester's (1983) sample, the highest-ranked reason in Raganella and White's (2004) study, and the most commonly cited motive for both San Diego Police Department applicants (Ridgeway et al., 2008) and criminal justice majors (Yim, 2009). In a related vein, a desire to serve was among the most highly rated reasons among California academy trainees (California Commission on POST, 2006). Although a social desirability bias might factor into the high ranking of public service to some degree, as public service might be viewed as the "right" reason to enter law enforcement, one recruit's comments on the survey suggest that at least for some, that ranking is sincere:

> I think officers should want to be cops to help others primarily and let the benefits be added additional bonuses to the job, not the other way around.

Good retirement and health benefits were also regarded as important reasons for working in law enforcement, and again, this reinforces results from previous studies. Low salaries have been blamed for recruiting challenges in several communities—San Diego and New York, for example (San Diego Police Department and Buck Consultants, 2006; Baker and Greenhouse 2008). However, we found that 87 percent of new recruits felt that the good salary was an important reason for them to pursue a policing career.

Job attributes such as power, authority, and a military-like structure were less compelling reasons for entering law enforcement. Moreover, few new recruits saw law enforcement as simply a stepping-stone
to some other opportunity or selected law enforcement because they
were out of options.

Key Group of Interest: Female Recruits

Figure 2.2 shows the average ratings of the reasons for pursuing law
enforcement careers for male and female recruits, excluding those reasons for which male and female recruits did not differ significantly. The
lines show the range of responses for 80 percent of the male or female
survey respondents, with the location of the circles marking the average response.

Consistent with Raganella and White's (2004) analysis of NYPD
academy recruits, women rated public service as a more important

Figure 2.2
**Gender Differences in Recruits' Reasons for Pursuing a Career in Law
Enforcement**

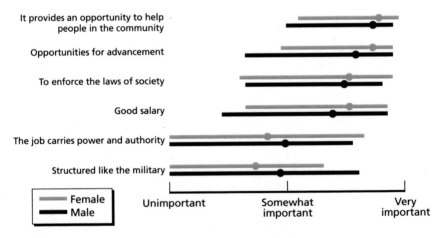

SOURCE: 2008–2009 RAND Law Enforcement Recruit Survey.
NOTES: The circles indicate the average response for males or females, and the lines
represent the range for 80 percent of the responses. For all survey items shown in
this figure, the average response for women was statistically significantly different
from the average response for men (p < 0.05).
RAND MG992-2.2

reason for their career choice than did men. This suggests that recruiting strategies that focus on public service may be not only attractive to male applicants, who constitute more than 80 percent of new recruits, but especially likely to be attractive to female applicants. Again corroborating Raganella and White's (2004) work, the female recruits also viewed a law enforcement career as good professional choice, as it offered them opportunities for advancement and a good salary. In a national survey of female police officers, Seklecki and Paynich (2007) found that public service was a primary motivation for entering law enforcement, but job security was the primary reason for staying in the job. We also found that reasons such as the power and authority inherent in the job and law enforcement's military structure were less likely to be motivating factors for women than men.

As noted in Chapter One, we also used regression analysis to examine whether different groups of recruits of potential interest to law enforcement recruiters (e.g., women, older recruits) viewed different reasons for entering law enforcement as more important when holding other characteristics constant. Table 2.1 summarizes the results of this analysis for each of the groups. Each row represents a regression model for which we used the variables listed in the columns to predict how respondents would quantify the importance of the factor in the row. An up arrow indicates that the reason (the row label) was more important for a particular group (column label) than for its counterpart, and a down arrow indicates that it was less important. Triangles replace the arrows when the effect is a particularly large difference between a particular group and its comparison group, specifically a change of 0.3 or greater on the 5-point Likert scale used for this survey item. For example, the female recruits regarded opportunities for advancement and good salary as more important reasons than did male recruits, and the upward-pointing triangle in the cell for good salary indicates that the difference between male recruits and female recruits in selecting this reason was especially large in magnitude. In addition, female recruits viewed the power and authority that the job carries as a less important reason than did male counterparts.

Table 2.1
Summary of Reasons for Entering Law Enforcement, by Key Group of Interest

General Reason	Specific Reason	Women	Asian	Black	Hispanic	Older Recruits (age 26+)	From Immigrant Family	Bachelor's Degree	Military Experience	Prior LE Experience
Public service	It provides an opportunity to help people in the community				↑		↑	↓		
	To fight crime				↑					↑
	To enforce laws of the society			↑				↓		↑
Benefits	Good salary	▲			↑					
	Good retirement plan									↓
	Good health insurance benefits								↓	
	Job security					↑				
Work environment	The excitement of the work		▲			↓				
	Structured like the military					↓			▲	↑
	You work on your own a lot; have a good deal of autonomy						↑		↑	▲
	The variety and nonroutine nature of the work									↑
	Good camaraderie with your co-workers							↓		
Professional qualities	The prestige of the profession			▲	↑		↑			↑
	Opportunities for advancement	↑			↑				↓	
	The job carries power and authority	▼					↑			
Other job options	To gain experience for another job		▲		▲	↓	↑			
	There was a lack of other job alternatives					↑			↑	
	Other job alternatives were not as interesting		▲			▼			▼	

SOURCE: 2008–2009 RAND Law Enforcement Recruit Survey.

Table 2.1—Notes

Arrows denote statistically meaningful relationships at $p < 0.05$. An up arrow indicates that the group, on average, rated a reason as more important than its reference group. A down arrow indicates that the group, on average, rated a reason as less important than its reference group. We replace the arrows with dark triangles (▲ ▼) to indicate respondent features associated with a change of at least 0.3 on the 5-point Likert scale. Reference groups are as follows: men (for women), white (for Asian, black, and Hispanic), younger recruits (for older recruits), recruits from nonimmigrant family (for those from an immigrant family), recruits with only a high school diploma (for those with a bachelor's degree), recruits who have no military experience or no prior law enforcement experience (for those who do).

Key Group of Interest: Minority Recruits

Turning our attention to minority recruits' reasons for entering law enforcement, we first note that departments often strive to maintain a composition that is reflective of the community. This can be challenging for a variety of reasons. For example, some groups, such as women, generally have a lower propensity to be interested in law enforcement careers. In addition, police efforts to encourage racially and ethnically diverse applicants can run into legal challenges. In California, for example, Proposition 209 prevents public agencies from actively shaping the racial/ethnic composition of their hires. This may include targeting recruiting activities to certain predominantly minority neighborhoods. Departments clearly need to avoid "New Haven Firefighter" practices—that is, the kind of practices that discard test results when the racial/ethnic composition of eligible recruits does not match targets. One survey respondent noted:

> It is offensive and blatantly racist to have answered so many surveys and questionnaires on one's ethnicity through the application and hiring process. It should not be a factor.

It is therefore an open question to what degree departments should actively focus recruiting efforts on certain racial/ethnic groups. We do not intend to address that question, but rather describe racial/ethnic differences so that those departments concerned about the diversity of their recruits can appreciate those differences.

As we did in our analysis of differences by gender, we first considered unadjusted differences in minority recruits' reasons for pursuing a career in law enforcement. As Figure 2.3 illustrates, the reasons

Figure 2.3
Racial/Ethnic Differences in Recruits' Reasons for Pursuing a Career in Law Enforcement

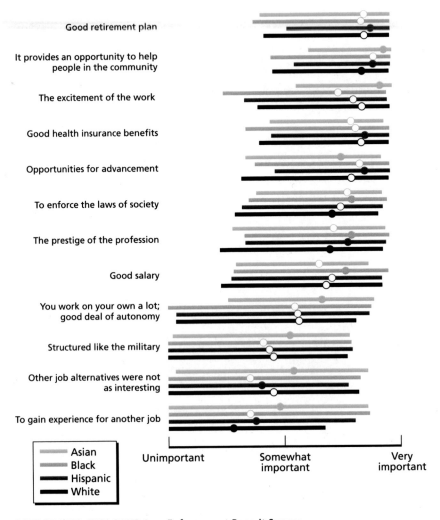

SOURCE: 2008–2009 RAND Law Enforcement Recruit Survey.
NOTES: The circles indicate the average response for that racial/ethnic group, and the lines represent the range for 80 percent of the responses. Filled-in circles indicate that the group reported significantly different ratings than the other groups (p < 0.05).
RAND MG992-2.3

for pursuing a law enforcement career varied substantially by race/ethnicity. The lines show the range of responses for 80 percent of the Asian, black, Hispanic, and white respondents. In addition, a filled-in circle indicates that a racial/ethnic group is statistically different from other groups. Such was particularly the case for Asian recruits, who differed significantly from other racial/ethnic groups on seven out of the 12 reasons.

Before describing those differences, it is important to note that Asian respondents are themselves a diverse group. The Asian portion of our survey sample (N=46) is 41 percent Korean, 23 percent Chinese, 16 percent Vietnamese, 8 percent Japanese, and 13 percent from another Asian country.[1] Almost all of them are first generation (23 percent) or immigrants themselves (69 percent). Asian respondents frequently cited community service as being a very important component of their career choice, but also were more likely to rank the job's excitement as a key reason.

Figure 2.3 also indicates that black recruits were significantly more likely to indicate that the job's prestige, enforcing society's laws, and a good salary were important factors. Hispanic recruits were attracted to the benefits package, the opportunities for advancement, and the prestige of the profession. Nonwhite recruits rated public service as more important than did white recruits. Relative to nonwhite recruits, white recruits viewed the prestige of the profession, the enforcement of society's laws, and the use of this job as a stepping-stone to another job as less important reasons for entering law enforcement.

Moving on to our regression analysis, in which we controlled for other respondent characteristics, Table 2.1 (on p. 20) shows that Asian, black, and Hispanic recruits all differed in some ways from their white counterparts in terms of their motivations. Asian recruits were significantly more likely to report that they entered law enforcement because of the excitement of the work, to gain experience for another job, and because other job alternatives were less interesting. The triangles in Table 2.1 denote that these differences between white and

---

[1]   Note that since our sample included 46 Asian respondents, these percentages are intended to give the reader a rough idea of those reporting race as Asian rather than precise estimates of, for example, Vietnamese recruits.

Asian survey respondents were particularly large. Black recruits as a whole emphasized a desire to enforce society's laws and the prestige of the profession, and the difference between black and white recruits was especially large for the latter reason. Hispanic recruits were more likely than white recruits to note entering law enforcement for several different public service reasons, because of the good salary, and, like black recruits, because of the prestige of the profession. Similar to Asian recruits, Hispanic recruits agreed much more strongly than white recruits that experience for another job was an incentive to pursue a career in policing.

While we focused on separate analyses of the differences between men and women and the differences across racial/ethnic groups, we also examined interactions between race/ethnicity and gender, and found one notable result. Table 2.2 lists the percentage of recruits that rated public service as more important than they did a good salary. For white and Hispanic recruits, men and women were nearly equally likely to rate public service as more important than they did salary. However, black women were significantly less likely than black men (or any other group for that matter) to rate public service as more important than salary.

Table 2.2
Percentage That Rated Public Service as More Important Than Salary, by Race/Ethnicity

Race/Ethnicity	Women	Men
White	54	51
Asian	61	82
Black	21	45
Hispanic	55	56

SOURCE: 2008–2009 RAND Law Enforcement Recruit Survey.

Other Key Groups of Interest

Table 2.1 also documents how other potential groups of interest differ in their motives for entering law enforcement. Older recruits rated job security significantly higher than those 25 or younger, and they also gave less emphasis to two aspects of law enforcement's work environment, its excitement and military-like structure. In addition, they were more likely than younger recruits to report that they went into law enforcement because of a lack of other alternatives. On the other hand, older recruits were less likely to report that their motivations included gaining experience for another job or that other job options were less interesting, and the difference between older and younger recruits regarding less interesting job alternatives was particularly large.

Compared with recruits not from immigrant families, those from immigrant families placed greater emphasis on law enforcement's professional qualities—its prestige and the power and authority inherent to the work. They also were more likely to regard helping others in the community, job autonomy, and the opportunity to gain experience for another job as important reasons for entering law enforcement.

Generally, those with a college education appeared less focused on the public service aspects of a law enforcement career than were the recruits with less education; they rated an opportunity to help people in the community and enforcing the law of society lower than did recruits with a high school education. In addition, camaraderie with one's co-workers was less likely to be valued by college graduates as a motive for pursuing a law enforcement career.

Finally, prior work experience accounted for some differences in recruits' reasons for seeking work as a police officer or deputy. Recruits who served in the military viewed two aspects of the work environment, its military-like structure and degree of autonomy, as more important than did recruits without this work experience. Not surprisingly, the difference between the two groups was especially pronounced for the military-like structure reason. Prior military recruits also gave greater emphasis to a lack of other job alternatives as a motivation. Conversely, they were less inclined to rate opportunities for advancement, good health insurance, and less interesting job alternative as important reasons.

Like those with prior military service, recruits with prior law enforcement experience tended to view the military-like structure of the work environment and the autonomy it affords as important reasons for pursuing a law enforcement career. The autonomy was particularly important to this group of recruits, and recruits with prior law enforcement experience also regarded work variety more highly than did those recruits without previous experience in law enforcement. Public service was another strong motivating factor for this group of recruits, as was the prestige of the profession. However, recruits with prior law enforcement experience were less inclined to view a good retirement plan as important.

Disadvantages of Law Enforcement Careers

We asked new recruits what disadvantages or cons about law enforcement came into mind when they were deciding whether to pursue a career in law enforcement. We provided them with a list of potential disadvantages and asked them to select as many as were applicable. Next, we asked them to think of a family member or friend close to them in age who did not pursue a law enforcement career and assess why he or she did not also pursue law enforcement. Although not as reliable as asking these peers directly to explain their lack of interest in law enforcement, we viewed responses to this questions as a type of "secondhand" information that could be informative for developing a strategy to target new applicants. Along these lines, the list for this second question included one option, criminal record, that was not applicable to recruits already screened and participating in a training academy yet potentially very relevant to family members or friends who declined to pursue a law enforcement career.

Figure 2.4 shows the responses to both of these questions. The darker bars indicate the percentage of recruits who indicated a particular disadvantage came to mind when they were making their own decision, and the lighter bars indicate the percentage of recruits who felt that a particular disadvantage deterred their family member or friend from pursing a law enforcement career. An asterisk indicates that there was a statistically significant difference between the two sets of views. Disadvantages are listed in Figure 2.4 in descending order based on the recruits' reporting of their peers' views.

Figure 2.4
Recruits' Perceptions of the Primary Disadvantages of a Law Enforcement Career

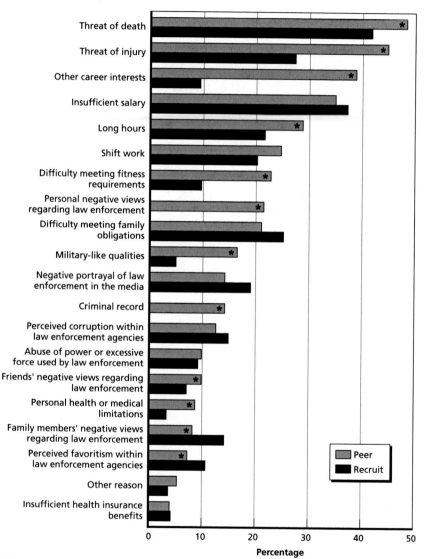

SOURCE: 2008–2009 RAND Law Enforcement Recruit Survey.
NOTES: Bars marked with an asterisk indicate statistically significant differences at p < 0.05. A criminal record option was not included in the question pertaining to recruits' own views.
RAND MG992-2.4

The most frequently cited reasons that recruits gave for why their peers did not enter law enforcement were threat of injury and threat of death. As shown in the figure, significantly more respondents identified these as concerns for their peers than for themselves. The difference in responses related to other career interests was even more pronounced; almost four times as many respondents indicated this was a deterrent for their peers than for themselves. Other factors that appeared to matter more for recruits' peers than for recruits themselves include long hours, perceived difficulty meeting fitness requirements, personal negative views regarding law enforcement, and law enforcement's military-like qualities. For each of these disadvantages, the proportion of recruits who felt it was a concern for their peers exceeded the proportion of recruits who had viewed it as a downside themselves. Conversely, issues of greater concern for recruits as a whole than for their peers (according to the recruits) included the family members' negative views regarding law enforcement and perceived favoritism within law enforcement agencies. Insufficient health benefits appeared to be of little concern for either group. Also of note, salary and benefits do not distinguish recruits from their non–law enforcement peers. This suggests that agencies are mostly battling other factors, most notably career interests, trends in physical fitness, and negative views of the police.

Key Group of Interest: Female Recruits

As with the reasons for entering law enforcement, we first consider actual differences between men and women in the survey responses and then present the results of the regression analysis, in which we controlled for other characteristics among respondents. Generally, women were more likely than men to perceive that physical fitness, family obligations, and favoritism in the police departments were cons of a law enforcement career. On the other hand, women were less likely to cite other career interests and insufficient salary as key barriers.

Table 2.3 summarizes the results of the regression analysis. An up arrow indicates that a reason was more important for a particular group than for its counterpart, and a down arrow indicates that it was less important. Triangles replace the arrows when the effect is a larger

Table 2.3
Summary of Disadvantages of Entering Law Enforcement, by Key Group of Interest

General Disadvantage	Specific Disadvantage	Women	Asian	Black	Hispanic	Older Recruits (age 26+)	From Immigrant Family	Bachelor's Degree	Military Experience	Prior LE Experience
Fears	Threat of injury									
	Threat of death						↓			
Benefits	Insufficient salary		▼			↓	↑	▲	↑	↑
	Insufficient health insurance benefits								▲	▲
Work environment	Long hours									
	Shift work		▼	↓		▲	↑			
	Military-like qualities, such as use of rank and command structure									
	Perceived favoritism within law enforcement agencies	▲								
Personal factors	Difficulty meeting family obligations	↑	▼							
	Difficulty meeting fitness requirements	▲		↑					▼	
	Personal health or medical limitations									
	Other career interests					▼	▲		▲	
External factors	Negative portrayal of law enforcement in the media					↓		↑		↑
	Friends' negative views regarding law enforcement			▲		▼				
	Family members' negative views regarding law enforcement			▲			↑			
	Perceived corruption within law enforcement agencies							↑		
	Abuse of power or excessive force used by law enforcement officer(s)								↑	

SOURCE: 2008–2009 RAND Law Enforcement Recruit Survey.

Table 2.3—Notes

Arrows denote statistically meaningful relationships at p < 0.05. An up arrow indicates that the group was more likely to select a disadvantage than its reference group. A down arrow indicates that the group was less likely to select a disadvantage than its reference group. We replace the arrows with dark triangles (▲ ▼) to indicate respondent features associated with at least a doubling (or halving) of the odds of indicating the given disadvantage. Reference groups are as follows: men (for women), white (for Asian, black, and Hispanic), younger recruits (for older recruits), recruits from nonimmigrant family (for those from an immigrant family), recruits with only a high school diploma (for those with a bachelor's degree), recruits who have no military experience or no prior law enforcement experience (for those who do).

difference between a particular group and its comparison group, specifically when the group's odds of selecting a particular disadvantage is less than half (a downward triangle) or more than double (an upward triangle) the odds for the reference group.

The table includes three notable differences between male and female recruits: Female recruits were more likely to cite perceived favoritism within law enforcement agencies as a disadvantage and to identify difficulties meeting family obligations and fitness requirements as barriers. The difference between male and female recruits was especially large for concerns related to perceived favoritism and fitness requirements.

Male and female recruits also relayed the barriers that their peers viewed as reasons why they did not become police officers or sheriff's deputies. We do not know the characteristics of their peers, beyond that recruits were asked to think of a friend or family member of similar age and are likely to have thought of a peer of the same gender. Once again, we first discuss actual differences between men and women in the survey responses, before moving on to discussion of our regression analysis of the data. Female recruits were more likely to indicate that their peers were deterred by a perceived lack of physical fitness. In addition, female recruits were more likely than male recruits to report that their peers held the perception that a law enforcement career might be incompatible with family obligations, with a gender gap in responses (18 percentage points) nearly equal to that for physical fitness. On the other hand, male recruits were more likely to perceive that their peers did not pursue law enforcement because of better salary prospects in other career fields. Consistent with the fact that men are more likely to have a criminal record, male recruits were twice as likely to cite their peers' criminal backgrounds as a barrier to a law enforcement career.

Table 2.4 summarizes the results of our regression analysis related to recruits' views of their peers on the disadvantages of a career in law enforcement. In these models, we use the characteristics of the recruits themselves to assess differences in their *peers'* responses. As noted previously, although we asked recruits to think of a friend or family member who is close in age, many of them might have selected a peer who differs from them in terms of race/ethnicity, sex, professional experience, and the other characteristics we are examining. As a result, this analysis does not precisely relate the peers' characteristics to the peers' reasons for not pursuing a law enforcement career. However, it is most likely that a recruit's characteristics are similar to their peers', so that we can use the recruit's characteristics as a "noisy" version of the peers'. Regression analyses in which characteristics are measured with error are more conservative—meaning that if we find significant differences using the recruits' characteristics here, then it is highly likely those differences would also be significant if we had the peers' true values.[2] While it is likely recruits cannot fully explain why their peers did not pursue law enforcement careers, recruits' secondhand accounts are a better source of information than what law enforcement recruiters currently have about people who are not considering law enforcement careers.

---

[2]   This is commonly referred to as "errors in variables" bias. In its simplest form, assume that p is the fraction of female respondents who reported for a female peer and q is the fraction of male respondents who reported for a male peer. Further assume that female peers have an average response m_F and male peers have an average response m_M. Because not all female respondents report for female peers, we will observe an average response from women equal to $pm_F + (1 - p)m_M$ and an average response from men equal to $qm_M + (1 - q)m_F$. The difference between the average responses for men and women can be written as

$$(p - (1 - q))(m_F - m_M).$$

Note that if $p = 1$ and $q = 1$, that is, all women report for female peers and likewise for men, then our reported difference between women and men would be correct, $m_F - m_M$. However, since we do not know whether the recruits reported for peers of the same sex but are quite certain that $p > 0.5$ and $q > 0.5$, the term $p - (1 - q)$ is between 0 and 1, which shrinks the reported difference. Therefore, any observed difference we report here would be larger if we were able to survey the peers directly.

Table 2.4
Summary of Peers' Perceived Disadvantages of Entering Law Enforcement, by Key Group of Interest

General Disadvantage	Specific Disadvantage	Women	Asian	Black	Hispanic	Older Recruits (age 26+)	From Immigrant Family	Bachelor's Degree	Military Experience	Prior LE Experience
Fears	Threat of injury									↓
	Threat of death									
Benefits	Insufficient salary	↓			↓		↑	▲		
	Insufficient health insurance benefits						↑		▲	
Work environment	Long hours	▲		↓				↑	↑	↑
	Shift work	↑	▼	↓				↑		
	Military-like qualities, such as use of rank and command structure								▲	
	Perceived favoritism within law enforcement agencies									
Personal factors	Difficulty meeting family obligations	▲		↓		▼				
	Difficulty meeting fitness requirements	▲				↓	↓			
	Personal health or medical limitations									
	Criminal record	▼				↓				
	Other career interests		▼	▼						
	Personal negative views regarding law enforcement			↑	↑					
External factors	Negative portrayal of law enforcement in the media									
	Friends' negative views regarding law enforcement		▲			▼			▲	
	Family members' negative views regarding law enforcement									
	Perceived corruption within law enforcement agencies					↓				
	Abuse of power or excessive force used by law enforcement officer(s)	↑				↓				

SOURCE: 2008–2009 RAND Law Enforcement Recruit Survey.

Table 2.4—Notes

Arrows denote statistically meaningful relationships at $p < 0.05$. An up arrow indicates that the group was more likely to select a disadvantage than its reference group. A down arrow indicates that the group was less likely to select a disadvantage than its reference group. We replace the arrows with dark triangles (▲ ▼) to indicate respondent features associated with at least a doubling (or halving) of the odds of indicating the given disadvantage. Reference groups are as follows: men (for women), white (for Asian, black, and Hispanic), younger recruits (for older recruits), recruits from nonimmigrant family (for those from an immigrant family), recruits with only a high school diploma (for those with a bachelor's degree), recruits who have no military experience or no prior law enforcement experience (for who that do).

Table 2.4 shows that, after adjusting for demographic differences among the respondents, female recruits still differed from male recruits in that they were more likely to report their peers' concerns about satisfying fitness requirements and meeting family obligations when they were considering a law enforcement career. In both cases, the difference between male and female recruits was notably large, indicating that these issues are especially salient to the women we surveyed and possibly their similar friends and family members as well. Women also were more inclined than men to note that their peers did not want to work in law enforcement because they viewed long hours and shift work as disadvantages. In addition, they tended to report that their peers viewed law enforcement officers' abuse of power or excessive force as a deterrent to a law enforcement career. Conversely, women were less likely to report that salary considerations or one's past might be a deterrent for their peers; men more strongly regarded both insufficient salary and a criminal record as reasons why their peers opted not to enter law enforcement.

Key Group of Interest: Minority Recruits

Our analysis of actual (i.e., unadjusted) survey responses revealed that racial/ethnic groups differed from one another in several key respects. Overall, nonwhite recruits were less likely to cite the shift work environment as one of the job's cons, but they were more likely to cite insufficient health benefits, difficulty meeting family obligations, and concerns about abuse of police power.

Black recruits were most exposed to their families' and friends' negative views of police, significantly more than other racial/ethnic groups. Nearly one-fourth of black recruits indicated that their family members in particular had negative views of the police and that this presented a barrier for them to pursue a law enforcement career. Asian recruits were much less likely to cite family obligations as a key barrier: Only 8 percent of Asian recruits cited family obligations as a barrier, compared with 23 to 25 percent of recruits from other racial/ethnic groups. Hispanic recruits closely resembled white recruits regarding perceived downsides to a law enforcement career.

Turning to the regression analysis, Table 2.3 shows that, even after other respondent characteristics were taken into account, Hispanic recruits were still no different from white recruits in terms of what they regarded as the disadvantages of a law enforcement career. However, Asian and black recruits differed significantly from white recruits in several ways. As noted before, Asian recruits were less likely to note that family obligations were a "con," and both Asian and black recruits were less likely to express reservations about shift work. Black recruits also placed less weight on salary as a disadvantage of law enforcement. However, black recruits were more likely to report having concerns about meeting fitness requirements when they were deciding on a law enforcement career, and they tended to identify friends' and family members' negative views regarding law enforcement as impediments. The latter is consistent with findings from focus groups conducted with minority officers serving in the Sacramento Police Department (Scrivner, 2006). Specifically, some noted that police officers are regarded unfavorably in minority neighborhoods, so minorities who choose this profession are viewed as "sell-outs" (Scrivner, 2006, p. 96).

Turning our attention to recruits' views of why their friends and family members did not make a similar career choice (and first discussing the unadjusted survey results), black and Hispanic recruits were generally the least likely to select barriers of any kind on their peers' behalf. In particular, relatively few black recruits perceived that their peers would have difficulty meeting the physical fitness requirements. Personal negative views about law enforcement were highest among Hispanic recruits. The peers of white recruits differed from the peers of nonwhite recruits in two key ways. First, they saw the policing work environment itself to be a key barrier, namely the long hours, the shift work, and its military-like qualities. Second, nearly 50 percent of white recruits' peers have other career interests. In contrast, the peers of non-white recruits were not as averse to policing's work environment and were less likely to have competing career interests as a major barrier.

Turning to our regression analysis, Table 2.4 shows that many of these differences persisted even after other respondent character-istics were taken into account. Specifically, white recruits were more likely than either Asian or black recruits to agree that shift work was an impediment for their peers, and they were more likely than black recruits to report that policing's long hours were a deterrent for their peers. In addition, white recruits were much more inclined than His-panic or black recruits to agree that other career interests were a reason why their friends or family members did not opt for a career in law enforcement.

The results of our regression analysis also indicated that Hispanic recruits were less inclined to cite insufficient salary as a downside for their peers, and black recruits were less likely to believe their peers did not enter law enforcement because it would make it difficult to attend to family responsibilities. On the other hand, both groups of recruits were more likely to report that their peers' negative views of law enforcement deterred them from pursuing a law enforcement career. Further, Asian recruits were much more likely than white recruits to note that their friends' negative views toward law enforcement were a deterrent.

Other Key Groups of Interest

The next group listed in Tables 2.3 and 2.4, recruits from immigrant families, perceived the disadvantages of law enforcement quite differ-ently than those whose families have been in the United States for several generations. They were less inclined to have concerns about the threat of death inherent in a career in law enforcement. Instead, during their decision process, recruits from immigrant families focused on insufficient salary, shift work, and their family members' negative views of law enforcement. In addition, they were much more likely to have considered other career interests. With respect to their peers' perceptions, recruits from immigrant families tended to report that their peers were deterred by perceptions of inadequate salary and health benefits. Conversely, they were less inclined to feel that their friends and family members viewed the fitness requirements as an obstacle.

Turning our attention to college graduates, this group of recruits was rather strong in its view that insufficient salary was a downside of law enforcement. They were much more likely than those without a college degree to identify it as a disadvantage and to report that their peers felt similarly. These recruits also were inclined to have thought about the negative portrayal of law enforcement by the media and perceived corruption within law enforcement during their decision process. Other factors college graduates tended to believe deterred their peers were perceived long hours and shift work.

The final recruit groups of interest, those with prior military or law enforcement experience, resembled college graduates in their view that insufficient salary was a disadvantage of working in law enforcement. Both groups of recruits were especially inclined to have considered inadequate health insurance benefits as a downside when making their career decision. In addition, recruits with prior law enforcement experience were more likely to indicate that the negative portrayal of law enforcement in the media was a downside. Recruits with prior military service tended to be concerned with perceived abuse of power or the use of excessive force in law enforcement and were especially mindful of other career interests. On the other hand, they were much less inclined to view law enforcement's fitness requirements as an impediment.

There were fewer significant findings related to peers' perceived disadvantages for recruits with prior experience in the military or law enforcement. Recruits with military service were more likely to note their peers perceived law enforcements' health benefits, long hours, and military-like qualities as downsides. Those with prior law enforcement experience were less likely to report their friends or family members regarded the threat of injury as a disadvantage, and were more likely to indicate they were deterred by the long hours perceived as inherent to law enforcement careers.

Discussion

In the survey, we asked new recruits to indicate both their primary reasons for entering law enforcement and what potential downsides they took into consideration when making their decisions. They also shared with us what they thought deterred family members or friends close to them in age from pursuing a career in law enforcement. Consistent with past research, recruits noted that job security and helping the community were key motivations for them to pursue a career in law enforcement. Older recruits (age 26 and up) placed greater emphasis on job security than did younger recruits. Female recruits, minority recruits, and those from immigrant families tended to focus on public service aspects of law enforcement more than other recruits did. For instance, Hispanic recruits were more likely than white recruits to rate helping others in the community and fighting crime as important reasons for entering law enforcement.

New recruits most frequently cited the threat of death or injury and insufficient salary as potential cons to working in law enforcement that came to mind during their decision process. Recruits from immigrant families, college graduates, those with military experience, and those with prior law enforcement experience were more likely to report that inadequate pay was a downside they reflected upon when considering whether to enter law enforcement, whereas older recruits were less inclined to do so. However, the downsides that deterred recruits' peers from pursuing a law enforcement career, as perceived by recruits themselves, differed somewhat. While recruits thought their family members and friends were swayed by competing career interests, just as many of the recruits themselves had been, survey respondents noted that their peers were especially averse to joining a law enforcement department out of fear of injury or death.

Women perceive the fitness requirements to be a larger barrier to joining than men perceive it to be. In some departments, certain elements of the physical abilities test—those that can be taught in the academy or those that have less bearing on most police work but have great gender disparities in pass rates—have been modified or dropped altogether to permit more women to advance in the recruiting process. For example, the Long Beach Police Department eliminated the dragging of a 150-pound dummy in its test (Raymond et al., 2005). While promoting general physical fitness among young women is a challenging effort and the subject of large government efforts, such as the Trial of Activity for Adolescent Girls program, creating a work environment that is also sensitive to or even accommodating of family obligations might further promote the inclusion of more women in law enforcement.

Strategies can also be customized to reach out to potential non-white applicants. Table 1.2 indicates that Hispanic recruits represent 25 percent of new recruits in the survey sample, far greater than their current representation in law enforcement (14 percent) and in the general population (15 percent). This suggests that, generally, barriers are impacting other racial/ethnic groups to a larger extent than they are for Hispanic recruits. Importantly, nonwhite recruits reported that their peers were not as averse to policing's work environment and were less likely to have competing career interests as a major barrier. Black recruits in particular noted that they were attracted to the profession's prestige and the good salary that the job offered. Asian recruits, on the other hand, noted that their non–law enforcement peers were captured by other career interests, suggesting that this may be the greatest barrier that departments face in trying to increase Asian representation among their ranks.

Law enforcement recruiting programs can utilize these findings to attract new recruits. For example, recruiting materials could emphasize public service aspects of law enforcement work. Our survey suggests that such a strategy, in addition to attracting men and whites to join, might be particularly effective for attracting women and minority candidates. Addressing perceived downsides of law enforcement work, particularly those based on inaccurate perceptions, could also be an effective recruiting approach. Perhaps most notably, nearly 50 percent of surveyed recruits indicated that their peers are not considering law enforcement because of the threats of injury and death. This finding suggests that the public perception of the threat of death is exaggerated. In a recent study (LaTourrette, Loughran, and Seabury, 2008), RAND researchers examined injury and fatality rates for police services, including correctional officers, and found that in 2005, although injuries to police officers and sheriff's deputies were common, the rate of fatalities was 14.5 fatalities per 100,000 officers. Although this is more than three times the national average and certainly more risky than the typical office job, it is on par with the fatality rates of construction workers and truck drivers (U.S. Department of Labor, 2009). A law enforcement agency's recruiting campaign may not be able to do much to blunt the other salient downsides of police work (e.g., competing career interests, long hours), but the actual risks of the job are something that could be clarified early on in the application process or in recruiting materials.

CHAPTER THREE

Who and What Influences Recruits' Career Decisions?

In Chapter Two, we described recruits' primary reasons for pursuing a career in law enforcement and what they viewed as potential deterrents to entering this career field—two sets of perceptions that likely influence an individual's career decision. In this chapter, we turn our attention to factors that exert more of an overt influence on one's career choice: recruits' family and friends and characteristics of the agency with which they ultimately accepted employment. Just as understanding recruits' motives for entering law enforcement and what they perceive as its downsides can inform recruiting strategies, so too may a heightened awareness of the external factors that potentially influence or lead to improved recruiting outcomes.

Influence of Family and Friends

Numerous studies have demonstrated that family, friends, and other acquaintances can be key influencers, positive and negative, on an individual's occupational choice. In addition, military researchers (e.g., Orvis, Sastry, and McDonald, 1996) have examined the role of key influencers, such as parents and friends, on potential enlistees' decision on whether to join the military. Accordingly, in our survey we included a question intended to reveal whether different individuals in new recruits' social networks may have influenced their decision to enter law enforcement. Given that past research (Ryan et al., 2001) found a relationship between police officer applicant views and family views of police work, we thought this line of inquiry could be especially informative for law enforcement recruiting. Note that since the sample includes only recruits, we do not know about the influencers who "successfully" dissuaded an applicant from actually joining a department.

Figure 3.1 describes these influencers and their opinions for the new recruits' career choice. The first column lists several potentially influential people with respect to the recruits' decision process. The second column gives the percentage of recruits who heard an opinion, solicited or unsolicited, from this potential influencer. For example, 78 percent of the recruits who completed our survey received some sort of opinion or advice from their biological fathers. In addition, we asked whether the potential influencer is or was involved in law enforcement. The third column shows these figures. Continuing the example for biological fathers, 30 percent of survey respondents indicated that their biological fathers are or were involved in law enforcement. Finally, we asked recruits to indicate whether the potential influencer's opinion was supportive of the recruit's decision to pursue a career in law enforcement. The fourth column shows the average for each opinion (the tick mark) as well as the range containing 80 percent of the responses (the line).

Overall, survey respondents most frequently indicated that their biological parents proffered an opinion about their plans to pursue a law enforcement career. Siblings and friends close in age were also mentioned by a majority of recruits (68 percent and 65 percent, respectively). Also of note, 50 percent of the recruits reported that they received an opinion from a law enforcement professional and that these professionals offer the strongest support for the decision. This corroborates Slater and Reiser's (1988) research, in which Los Angeles Police Department recruits indicated that police officers were among the most important sources of information about positions in that department. Along those lines, one recruit explained at the end of his survey:

> I ran into a police officer at a job fair who was extremely informative and answered many of my questions and concerns. He helped me assure myself I was making a great decision.

**Figure 3.1
Influencers of Recruits' Decision to Pursue a Law Enforcement Career**

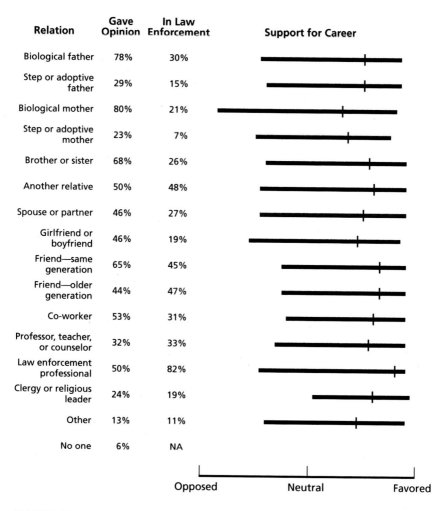

Relation	Gave Opinion	In Law Enforcement	Support for Career
Biological father	78%	30%	
Step or adoptive father	29%	15%	
Biological mother	80%	21%	
Step or adoptive mother	23%	7%	
Brother or sister	68%	26%	
Another relative	50%	48%	
Spouse or partner	46%	27%	
Girlfriend or boyfriend	46%	19%	
Friend—same generation	65%	45%	
Friend—older generation	44%	47%	
Co-worker	53%	31%	
Professor, teacher, or counselor	32%	33%	
Law enforcement professional	50%	82%	
Clergy or religious leader	24%	19%	
Other	13%	11%	
No one	6%	NA	

Opposed   Neutral   Favored

SOURCE: 2008–2009 RAND Law Enforcement Recruit Survey.
NOTE: The tick marks indicate the average response, and the lines represent the
range for 80 percent of the responses.
RAND MG992-3.1

In general, most potential influencers offered neutral to supportive opinions, with some small differences. For example, mothers were slightly less supportive than fathers, and the nature of their support varied more.

In the survey, we also posed a question about the factors that influenced recruits to accept employment at the agency that had sent them to the training, and the responses to that item are summarized in Figure 3.2. As with the recruits' decisions to pursue law enforcement careers (as previously shown in Figure 2.1), job benefits figured highly in recruits' decision to select a specific agency. Although the response options were somewhat different, the results are consistent with those reported by the California Commission on POST (2006). Specifically, in both surveys, the agency's reputation and assignment variety were among the most important reasons. Retirement plans and benefits were also regarded as important by both groups of survey respondents, although they were slightly more important to respondents in our sample.

Lim and his colleagues (2009) cited the long application process as a key barrier for effective recruiting at the Los Angeles Police Department. However, Figure 3.2 indicates that time-to-academy is distinctly lower in importance than numerous other factors for our national sample of large departments. The variability in the importance rating of time-to-academy is likely related to the variation in the processing time at the agencies surveyed. Comments from survey respondents provide insights about this variability. Several of the surveyed recruits found their recruiting processes to be long, tiresome, and mysterious, as the follow remark illustrates:

> I've also noticed a lack in communication with some agencies. After initial application and testing phases, I would sometimes go months without knowing what was going on or where I was in the process.

In a related vein, another recruit's experience with a timely process was a key factor in her decision:

Figure 3.2
Factors Influencing Recruits' Decision to Accept Employment at Their Agency

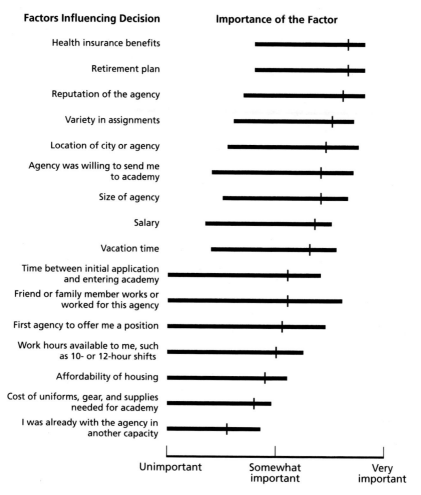

SOURCE: 2008–2009 RAND Law Enforcement Recruit Survey.
NOTE: The tick marks indicate the average response, and the lines represent the range for 80 percent of the responses.
RAND *MG992-3.2*

What helped me to choose the law enforcement agency I am currently with was the quick and thorough process compared to other agencies I applied to around the same time.

Key Group of Interest: Female Recruits

As in the preceding chapter, we considered gender-based differences in survey responses, both before and after adjusting for differences in other respondent characteristics. Figure 3.3 shows that, when deciding which particular agency to join, women were more likely than men to rate salary and vacation time as being important and less likely to rate the retirement plan as being important. Men were more likely to note that they took the first policing job offered to them.

Regression analysis highlighted additional ways that men and women varied in what they viewed as influencing their decision to select a particular law enforcement organization. The results of this analysis for all recruit groups of interest are provided in Table 3.1. An up arrow indicates that a reason was more important for a particular

Figure 3.3
Gender Differences in the Factors Influencing Recruits' Decision to Accept the Job Offer

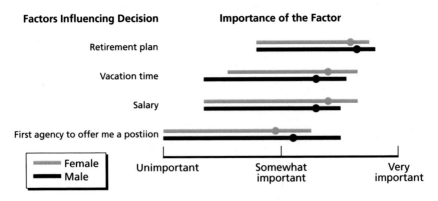

SOURCE: 2008–2009 RAND Law Enforcement Recruit Survey.
NOTES: The circles indicate the average response for males or females, and the lines represent the range for 80 percent of the responses. For all survey items shown in this figure, the average response for women was statistically significantly different from the average response for men (p < 0.05).
RAND MG992-3.3

Table 3.1
Summary of Factors Influencing the Decision to Accept the Job Offer, by Key Group of Interest

General Factor	Specific Factor	Women	Asian	Black	Hispanic	Older Recruits (age 26+)	From Immigrant Family	Bachelor's Degree	Military Experience	Prior LE Experience
Benefits	Salary	↑	↑	↑				↓		
	Retirement plan	↓			↑	↑			↓	
	Health insurance benefits								↓	
	Vacation time	↑							↓	
	Agency was willing to send me to academy						▼			
	Cost of uniforms, gear, and supplies needed for academy						↑			
Offer timing	First agency to offer me a position									
	Time between initial application and entering academy					↑				
Familiarity with the agency	Reputation of the agency		▼						▼	
	I was already with the agency in another capacity						↑			▲
	Friend or family member works or worked for this agency				▲		▼		▼	
Work environment	Variety in assignments			↓			↓			▲
	Work hours available to me, such as 10- or 12-hour shifts							↓		
Agency and community factors	Location of city or agency									
	Size of agency								↓	↑
	Affordability of housing			▲	↑		↑			

SOURCE: 2008–2009 RAND Law Enforcement Recruit Survey.

Table 3.1—Notes

Arrows denote statistically meaningful relationships at $p < 0.05$. An up arrow indicates that the group, on average, rated a factor as more important than its reference group. A down arrow indicates that the group rated a factor as less important than its reference group. We replace the arrows with dark triangles (▲ ▼) to indicate respondent features associated with a change of at least 0.3 on the 5-point Likert scale. Reference groups are as follows: men (for women), white (for Asian, black, and Hispanic), younger recruits (for older recruits), recruits from nonimmigrant family (for those from an immigrant family), recruits with only a high school diploma (for those with a bachelor's degree), recruits who have no military experience or no prior law enforcement experience (for those who do).

group than for its counterpart, and a down arrow indicates that it was less important. Triangles replace the arrows when the effect is a larger difference between a particular group and its comparison group, specifically a change of 0.3 or greater on the 5-point Likert scale used for this survey item. Female recruits' higher ratings of salary and vacation time persisted even after other demographics were taken into account, whereas a new finding related to male recruits' preferences emerged. Specifically, men were more likely than women to agree that the retirement plan offered by their employing agency was a factor in their decision to accept a job offer.

Key Group of Interest: Minority Recruits

As shown in Table 3.1, both Asian and black recruits were more likely than white recruits to agree that salary was an important factor. Black recruits also placed greater emphasis on the affordability of housing and were less inclined to agree that the agency's reputation or the possibility of variety in job assignments played a role in their decision. Hispanic recruits resembled black recruits in valuing the affordability of housing. They also were more likely than white recruits to identify as important factors the agency's retirement plan, the time between their initial application and entering academy, and having a friend or family member with employment experience at the same agency. As the triangle in the table signifies, this last reason was especially important for Hispanic recruits compared with white recruits.

Other Key Groups of Interest

Table 3.1 reveals one age-based difference in factors that influenced recruits to accept their employing agency's job offer: Not surprisingly, older recruits placed greater emphasis on the agency's retirement plan. Recruits from immigrant families varied considerably from those from nonimmigrant families. They were more likely to identify the cost of materials needed for academy, the affordability of housing, and their own affiliation with the agency as important factors, and less likely to indicate that the agency's willingness to send them to academy, having friends or family members affiliated with the agency, or variety in assignments were important considerations.

Consistent with their tendency to regard the salaries available to law enforcement personnel as a disadvantage of the career field, college graduates were less likely than recruits with less education to note that salary played an important part in their decision to accept a particular job offer. They were also less inclined to rate the work hours available to them as important. Recruits with prior military service placed less emphasis on the benefits available from their employing agency and their familiarity with the agency (e.g., agency reputation) when deciding to accept the offer, and they also paid little mind to the size of the agency. As suggested by the triangles in Table 3.1, recruits with military service were much less likely than those without military service to indicate that agency familiarity played an important role in their decision. Conversely, recruits with prior law enforcement were much more inclined than those without this work experience to regard agency familiarity—namely, their existing affiliation with the agency—as an important factor in their decision. Recruits with prior law enforcement experience also gave higher ratings to variety in work assignments and the agency's size.

Role of Victimization on Law Enforcement Career Choices

We also asked new recruits whether personal experiences of crime victimization, either having been a victim themselves or having their family or friends victimized, influenced their decision to pursue a law enforcement career. Table 3.2 shows that crime victimization was an important factor for some new recruits. For recruits at large U.S. agencies, 31 percent indicated that victimization was at least somewhat important.[1]

Table 3.2
The Influence of Victimization on the Decision to Join

Level of Influence	Percentage
Pursued law enforcement career because I had friends/relatives who were crime victims	
Very important	17
Somewhat important	11
Unimportant	20
Friends/family have not been victims	51
Pursued law enforcement career because I was a crime victim	
Very important	11
Somewhat important	7
Unimportant	16
Have not been a victim	66

SOURCE: 2008–2009 RAND Law Enforcement Recruit Survey.

Discussion

Mothers and fathers are key influencers on the decision to pursue a law enforcement career; approximately 80 percent of new recruits reported that parents gave an opinion on their career choice. The majority of recruits also identified siblings and friends close in age as opinion sources. Police officers frequently give very strong support, and half of new recruits reported discussing their decisions with law enforcement professionals. Outreach strategies that address key influencers might

---

[1]   Many recruits noted both their own victimization and that of a family member or friend as important, so the 31 percent figure noted here cannot be directly computed from Table 3.2.

improve recruiting efforts. Such strategies could focus on educating parents about law enforcement careers and on connecting prospective recruits with law enforcement professionals. For example, agencies could develop a brochure for parents or a short video, viewable on the agency's website, that portrays the realities of the profession and expressly addresses misconceptions.

Other recruiting strategies may be informed by the agency and job characteristics that recruits viewed as important influences on their decision to accept employment at a particular law enforcement agency. The agency's health insurance benefits and retirement plan were the most important factors, on average, among the recruits surveyed. Hispanic recruits and older recruits rated retirement plans as more important than did white recruits and younger recruits, respectively. The agency's reputation and the potential for a variety of assignments also were widely regarded as important decision factors. Although not highly rated overall, the affordability of housing was an important factor for black recruits, Hispanic recruits, and those from immigrant families. Recruiter efforts to highlight how their agency is superior to other departments, particularly those with whom they are competing for new hires, may influence prospective police officers or sheriff's deputies to accept employment at their agency.

CHAPTER FOUR

Recruiting Strategies

Overview

This chapter focuses directly on law enforcement agencies' recruitment practices—both the effectiveness of strategies in use at the time of our survey and recruits' views of the potential effectiveness of different actions and incentives. While a number of studies have examined recruitment strategies from the perspective of the recruiter or the agency (e.g., Taylor et al., 2005; California Commission on POST, 2006; Whetstone, Reed, and Turner, 2006; Wilson and Grammich, 2009), few have approached the issue from the eyes of the prospective candidate or current recruit.

To start, Figure 4.1 shows what first prompted recruits to contact the agency that they ultimately joined (respondents could select more than one item). The results indicate that friends and family in law enforcement were extremely influential in directing new recruits to a particular agency. This differs somewhat from a survey of California training academy students (California Commission on POST, 2006); only 26 percent of them indicated they were recruited to their agency via a referral from an agency employee who was a friend of relative. But our results are consistent with the views of law enforcement recruiters from across the country, who in a 2005 survey rated referrals from friends or relatives currently employed at their agency as one of the top ways that qualified candidates were attracted to their agency (California Commission on POST, 2006). All in all, this finding should encourage departments to use their own officers and civilian staff to cultivate new recruits.

Figure 4.1
Sources and Influences That Motivated Recruits' Application to Current Agency

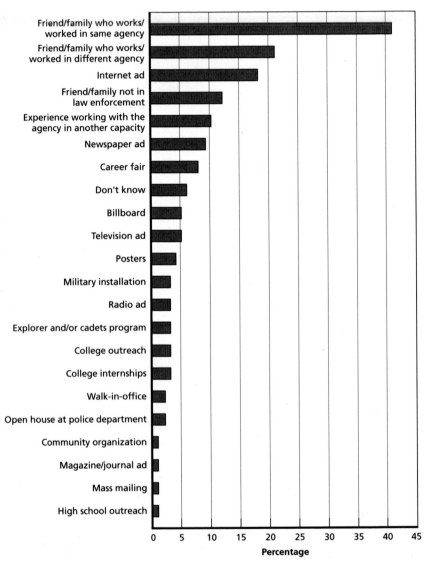

SOURCE: 2008–2009 RAND Law Enforcement Recruit Survey.
RAND MG992-4.1

Among advertising outlets, Internet advertising, one of the most frequently used recruitment methods reported by agencies themselves (Taylor et al., 2005), was the only form to register more than a 10 percent response from the overall sample. This may because other forms of advertising are simply not used as frequently as the Internet. One new recruit noted:

> The [department] website was a great tool when I was researching the position. There was much more information at this site than many of the other law enforcement sites I visited.

Other survey results suggest that the Internet has greater potential as an advertising tool than the responses to this question may indicate. Specifically, as shown in Figure 4.2, the majority of recruits who participated in our survey use the Internet extensively. Over 50 percent reported daily use or more, and just under 30 percent access the Inter-

Figure 4.2
Frequency of Recruits' Internet Usage in the Past Year

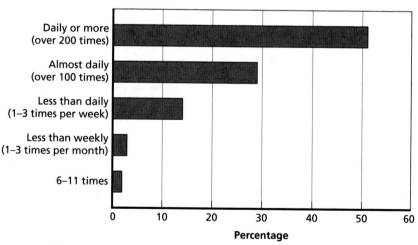

SOURCE: 2008–2009 RAND Law Enforcement Recruit Survey.
NOTE: The following options were also listed but were not selected by any respondents: "did not access within the past year," "once or twice," or "3–5 times."
RAND MG992-4.2

net almost daily. Conversely, no survey respondents indicated that they used the Internet less than six times per year.

We not only asked recruits how frequently they use the Internet, but also inquired about *how* they use it. The Internet has grown exponentially in terms of applications and websites, so additional data on what recruits actually do when they are online may help law enforcement agencies make the most of what typically are limited recruiting funds. Figure 4.3 summarizes the responses to this question and shows that almost all the recruits surveyed (95 percent) use the Internet for email. Seventy-five percent of recruits also indicated conducting online information searches. Perhaps of greater interest to law enforcement recruiters, 55 percent of respondents conducted job searches online as well. These results suggest that law enforcement agencies should not only maintain a website that represents their organization, but should also consider promoting their agency in other online outlets. For example, job listings could be posted on Internet job boards (e.g., Monster. com, CareerBuilder.com), and an agency presence could be developed and maintained at little cost on social networking sites such as Face-

Figure 4.3
How New Recruits Use the Internet

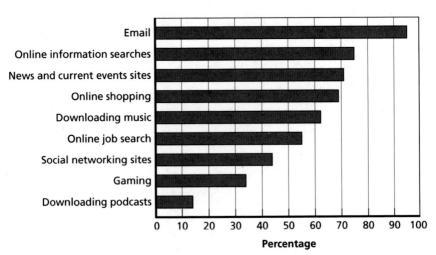

SOURCE: 2008–2009 RAND Law Enforcement Recruit Survey.
RAND *MG992-4.3*

book or MySpace, which 44 percent of recruits reported accessing. Finally, given the ubiquity of email, agencies could coordinate with local sources of prospective candidates, such as military installations, colleges, and universities, to send out mass emails regarding job opportunities. This may be a low-cost, effective way to reach groups of high-quality recruits, such as criminal justice majors and personnel separating from the military.

Figure 4.1 also indicates that relatively few recruits indicated that television, radio, billboard, or newspaper advertisements were the first prompt for them to consider the agency that they ultimately joined. However, in some communities, television advertising appeared to be a potentially important resource for attracting some recruits; for seven of the agencies that we surveyed, more than 10 percent of their new recruits were first prompted by a television advertisement. This suggests that effective television ad placement might enhance recruiting in some communities, but not all.

There were few differences between men and women on what first prompted them to consider a law enforcement career. One key difference is that women were almost twice as likely as men to indicate that working for the agency in another capacity was what initially generated their interest in being an officer (16 percent for women versus 9 percent for men). This suggests that a key strategy for expanding the presence of women among sworn ranks could be to introduce them to law enforcement careers through civilian jobs in the department. Almost no women indicated that traditional advertising outlets (e.g., newspaper, radio) prompted them to consider a law enforcement career. There were no differences between men and women on being first prompted by the Internet.

We asked new recruits to advise us on what might improve recruiting in their law enforcement agency. A list of possible actions and incentives was provided, and survey respondents were instructed to use a 5-point scale to rate how effective or ineffective each strategy might be. Figure 4.4 provides their responses, with benefits again topping the list. However, as results discussed in Chapter Three indicate, new recruits are already generally pleased with the benefits they have been offered by their employer. Given that recruits viewed insufficient

Figure 4.4
Recruits' Perceptions of the Effectiveness of Recruiting Strategies

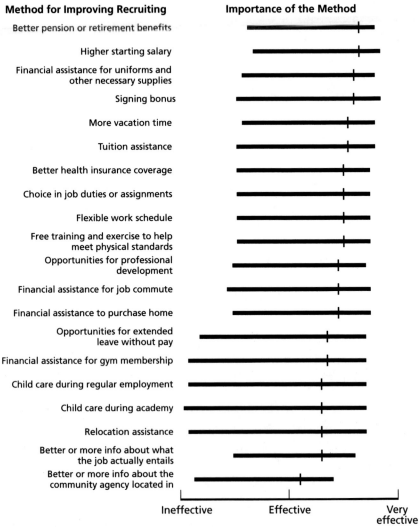

SOURCE: 2008–2009 RAND Law Enforcement Recruit Survey.
NOTE: The tick marks indicate the average response, and the lines represent the range for 80 percent of the responses.
RAND MG992-4.4

salaries as a potential downside of pursuing a career in law enforcement (from Chapter Two), it is not surprising that such financial incentives as a higher starting salary, financial assistance for uniforms, and a signing bonus were also widely regarded by recruits as effective ways to improve recruiting outcomes at their agency. Not surprisingly, no action or incentive was viewed as ineffective on average, although the range of responses for some actions, such as financial assistance for a gym membership and child care, indicates that a notable proportion of the survey sample felt such tactics would not be effective.

Key Group of Interest: Female Recruits

Although there was little variation in the overall sample (i.e., recruits tended to rate most of the actions and incentives as effective or very effective), as shown in Table 4.1, we did observe variation among recruit groups of interest after adjusting their responses for differences in respondent characteristics. As in similar tables provided in earlier chapters, arrows denote both the presence of a statistically significant difference and the direction of the difference. For example, an upward arrow means a particular group deemed a specific strategy as more effective than did its comparison group. Triangles signify a difference of a greater magnitude. Turning our attention first to differences based on gender, women tended to give lower effectiveness ratings than men to three types of recruiting strategies: higher starting salaries, financial assistance for gym memberships, and financial assistance for purchasing a home. Female recruits' tendency to focus on public service aspects of law enforcement rather than its pecuniary benefits, discussed in Chapter Three, may help explain these findings. Similarly, we also noted in Chapter Three that women were more likely than men to express concerns about meeting agency fitness requirements; in a related vein, female recruits were more likely than male recruits to agree that free training and exercise to help meet physical standards could be a highly effective recruiting strategy.

Key Group of Interest: Minority Recruits

Black recruits did not differ in any way from white recruits in their opinions on the effectiveness of various recruiting strategies, but dis-

Table 4.1
Summary of Perceived Recruiting Strategy Effectiveness, by Key Group of Interest

General Strategy	Specific Strategy	Women	Asian	Black	Hispanic	Older Recruits (age 26+)	From Immigrant Family	Bachelor's Degree	Military Experience	Prior LE Experience
Financial incentives	Higher starting salary	↓				↓		▲		
	Signing bonus						↓	▲	↑	
	Better pension or retirement benefits				↑	↓				
	Better health insurance coverage				↑					
Financial assistance	Financial assistance for uniforms and other necessary supplies		▼						↓	
	Financial assistance for gym membership	↓			▲	↓		▲		
	Financial assistance to purchase home	↓	▼			↓				↑
	Financial assistance for job commute		▼			↓				
Other assistance	Relocation assistance					↓				↑
	Tuition assistance		▼			↓		↑		↑
	Child care during academy									
	Child care during regular employment									
	Free training and exercise to help meet physical standards	↑			↑	↓			↓	↑
Better information	Better or more info about what the job actually entails				↑					
	Better or more info about the community agency located in				▲					
Improved work environment	Opportunities for professional development				▲					▲
	Flexible work schedule						↑	▲		
	Choice in job duties or assignments					↓		▲	↑	↑
Better leave options	More vacation time					↓	↑			
	Opportunities for extended leave without pay						↑			

SOURCE: 2008–2009 RAND Law Enforcement Recruit Survey.

Table 4.1—Notes

Arrows denote statistically meaningful relationships at p < 0.05. An up arrow indicates that the group rated a possible strategy as more effective than its reference group. A down arrow indicates that the group rated a possible strategy as less effective than its reference group. We replace the arrows with dark triangles (▲ ▼) to indicate respondent features associated with a change of at least 0.3 on the 5-point Likert scale. Reference groups are as follows: men (for women), white (for Asian, black, and Hispanic), younger recruits (for older recruits), recruits from nonimmigrant family (for those from an immigrant family), recruits with only a high school diploma (for those with a bachelor's degree), recruits who have no military experience or no prior law enforcement experience (for those who do).

tinct patterns emerged for Asian and Hispanic recruits. As denoted by the triangles in Table 4.1, Asian recruits were considerably less inclined than white recruits to believe that several financially oriented strategies, including tuition assistance, would be effective. On the other hand, Hispanic recruits were more inclined to rate as highly effective several strategies of a pecuniary nature: better pension or retirement benefits, better health benefits, and financial assistance for a gym membership. Like female recruits, Hispanic recruits tended to feel that free support to help meet physical standards would be effective. Hispanic recruits were also more inclined than white recruits to believe that information-oriented strategies would be highly effective, and were more positive about the potential usefulness of providing opportunities for professional development.

Other Key Groups of Interest

Older recruits tended to view a wide variety of different recruiting strategies as less effective than did their younger contemporaries (age 25 and under). They include a number of financially oriented strategies, including a higher starting salary and various forms of financial assistance. As a whole, older recruits also gave lower effectiveness ratings to relocation assistance, tuition assistance, training and exercise programs to help meet physical standards, choice in job duties or assignments, and more vacation time. There were no strategies that older recruits tended to regard as more effective than did younger recruits.

Recruits from immigrant families were less likely than recruits from nonimmigrant families to view a signing bonus as highly effective. Instead, their responses suggested an emphasis on flexibility-related strategies: flexible work hours, more vacation time, and opportunities for extended leave without pay.

Not surprisingly, given earlier findings related to college graduates' views on law enforcement salaries, recruits with a bachelor's degree were much more likely than less educated recruits to believe that higher starting salaries and signing bonuses could be highly effective recruiting strategies. In a related vein, they also rated as more effective strategies involving financial assistance for gym memberships and tuition assistance. College graduates were considerably more likely to agree that strategies related to an improved work environment, such as choice in job duties or assignments, were effective.

Finally, prior work experience also helped to account for differences in perceptions of recruiting strategy effectiveness. Recruits who served in the military tended to view a signing bonus and choice in job duties or assignments as more effective recruiting tools than did recruits lacking this type of work experience. Recruits with military service as a whole gave lower ratings to two strategies, financial assistance for uniforms and other supplies and free support to help meet physical standards. Recruits with prior law enforcement experience tended to give higher effectiveness ratings to a number of strategies: financial assistance for a home purchase, relocation assistance, tuition assistance, free support to help meet physical standards, opportunities for professional development, and choice in job duties or assignments. Perhaps these recruits' exposure to the law enforcement environment has made them more optimistic about the potential usefulness of these strategies.

Discussion

When asked to identify what first prompted them to consider working as a police officer or sheriff's deputy in their current law enforcement agency, recruits most frequently cited friends and relatives in law enforcement, particularly those working in the same agency. Accordingly, an agency's own officers and other staff may serve as an effective recruiting tool. The Internet was the most frequently mentioned advertising outlet, selected by 18 percent of the overall sample as an information source that motivated them to contact their current employer. Additional findings pertaining to Internet usage suggest that it may be a promising resource for law enforcement recruiters: 80 percent of recruits surveyed access the Internet almost daily or even more often, and the majority of them use the Internet for online information searches and online job searches. A large proportion (44 percent) also reported visit social networking sites, which provide a low-cost way for agencies to maintain an online presence in addition to or instead of an agency website.

Recruits also evaluated what incentives and actions might improve recruiting for their current law enforcement agency. On average, such financial incentives as a better pension, higher starting salary, financial assistance for uniforms and other supplies, and a signing bonus were deemed most effective. Yet, other strategies, including nonpecuniary ones, appeared to be important to particular groups of recruits. Women, Hispanic recruits, younger recruits, and those with prior law enforcement experience rated free training and exercise programs to help meet physical standards as more effective than their reference group. Similarly, college graduates, recruits with military experience, and those with prior law enforcement experience tended to view choice in job duties or assignments as more effective. While offering prospective recruits more compensation, either in the form of pay or benefits, may help attract qualified candidates, these results suggest that other, potentially less costly strategies can also be used to target specific types of recruits.

CHAPTER FIVE
Conclusions and Recommendations

Recruiting new police officers and sheriff's deputies at the start of the 21st century was a challenging and expensive operation. Even with large investments in recruiting, departments struggled to fill their ranks to meet the demand for police services and to replace separating officers. Although the recession that began in December 2007 greatly increased the labor supply and reduced cities' appetites for hiring, trends indicate that this is a lull in what will likely be a long-term challenge to hire and retain quality law enforcement personnel.

This study surveyed the newest generation of law enforcement recruits, those hired and entering training academies in the 2008–2009 timeframe, and it marks the first instance, at least in recent years, that a nationally representative sample of recruits from major municipal law enforcement agencies participated in a recruiting-oriented survey. In times of economic prosperity and tight labor markets, the responses of these recruits offer strategies for departments to be more competitive in attracting new personnel. Regardless of the economic conditions, a better understanding of new recruits can help agencies target candidates who likely will be satisfied with and have reasonable expectations of a law enforcement career, ultimately resulting in law enforcement professionals who are more easily retained.

Survey results indicate that recruits frequently chose a career in law enforcement for job security or to help the community, with groups including black recruits, Hispanic recruits, and those from immigrant families placing a greater emphasis on public service aspects of law enforcement than other recruits. Not surprisingly, insufficient salary was among the most frequently cited downsides of a law enforcement career, especially for college graduates and recruits with prior law enforcement experience. The recruits surveyed also indicated that their peers did not enter law enforcement primarily because of competing career interests and the threat of injury or death associated with law enforcement.

Survey responses also revealed the influence of not only mothers and fathers on the decision to pursue a career in law enforcement, but also siblings and friends close in age. Law enforcement professionals played a prominent role in influencing many recruits' decision to enter law enforcement. Moreover, recruits most frequently indicated that friends and relatives in law enforcement, particularly in the same agency, first prompted them to consider working at their current law enforcement agency. After the decision to work in law enforcement was made, factors that motivated the recruits we studied to accept employment at their current agency included health insurance benefits and retirement plans. The agency's reputation and the possibility to work on a variety of assignments were also mentioned by large proportions of the overall survey sample. Although not highly rated on average, the affordability of housing was an important consideration for black recruits, Hispanic recruits, and those from immigrant families.

Recruits also provided feedback on different strategies that might be effective in improving recruiting outcomes for their employer. Overall, financial incentives, such as a higher starting salary and signing bonus, were viewed as most effective, but other strategies emerged as important to different types of recruits. For example, women and Hispanic recruits were among those who rated free training and exercise programs to help meet physical standards as more effective, and college graduates were one of several groups of recruits who placed greater emphasis on the value of choice in job duties or assignments.

Overall, the experiences and opinions that recruits shared through their survey responses can inform the development of recruiting strategies. We conclude this report by highlighting some of those strategies, along with other recommendations that can be gleaned from the respondents.

Target the Perceptions of Would-Be Recruits and Their Potential Influencers

Survey results show how powerful recruits' own perceptions and those of key influencers, such as family and friends, can be in influencing the decision to enter law enforcement. For example, the prestige of the profession was a draw for some recruits, including black recruits, Hispanic recruits, those from immigrant families, and those with prior law enforcement experience in particular. Conversely, family's negative views regarding law enforcement were seen as a downside to entering law enforcement, especially for black recruits and those from immigrant families. Further, perceptions of the threat of injury or death related to working in law enforcement were viewed by recruits as a primary reason why their similarly aged peers did not follow the same career path.

These findings suggest that law enforcement agencies should endeavor to shape these perceptions about law enforcement careers, not only among prospective recruits, but also among people well situated to influence the next generation of police officers and sheriff's deputies. Efforts to enhance the prestige of the profession, such as by publicly recognizing the achievements of individual officers as well as agency-level successes, are one way to accomplish this. Another potential strategy is to employ public messages transmitted via different media (e.g., television, Internet) to both acknowledge and address negative views regarding law enforcement. Using a diverse group of real officers or deputies to talk about the realities of their profession, why they do it, and its rewards may be especially effective in shaping views of law enforcement held by prospective candidates or their family members.

In addition, law enforcement recruiting professionals may influence the perceptions of prospective candidates so that they not only want to pursue a career in law enforcement, but do so at the professional's own department, by pointing out how the department favorably compares with other employment options. Social psychology research is rife with evidence on how an individual's choice of referent, or *comparison other*, can affect his or her perspective. Accordingly, with the right basis for comparison, an agency's characteristics or aspects of the job itself may be viewed in a more favorable light. For example, the starting salary offered by a specific agency may not be as readily deemed insufficient if it is greater than other local alternatives and recruits are provided with the information necessary to make such a comparison. For example, a department such as Chicago's could note that its starting salary ($43,000) is competitive with other occupations in the city, such as mail carriers ($37,000), teachers ($44,000), and paralegals ($45,000) as well as with starting law enforcement salaries in nearby communities, such as Joliet ($43,000), and then note that the salary increases (to $58,000) by 18 months. Similarly, certain groups of recruits were concerned about the affordability of housing when deciding where to work. If the average price of housing is lower in communities near a particular agency than for those near its competitors, this may be a basis for comparison about which recruiters should educate prospective candidates.

A third perception-related technique is to correct misperceptions held by would-be candidates and their sphere of influence more generally. For example, while the threats of injury or death may loom large in the minds of recruits' peers, and perhaps in those of recruits' parents and other influencers, the reality is that, in recent years, police officers have had lower fatality rates than farmers, truck and taxi drivers, construction workers, and bartenders (U.S. Department of Labor, 2009). While policing is more dangerous than the average job, the safety record of modern policing deserves greater recognition. Accordingly, touting the profession's safety record and safety practices via public announcements, parents' brochures, and other instruments might increase the pool of interested candidates by correcting their perceptions and those of the people closest to them.

Recognize the Value of Both Financial and Nonfinancial Motivators

Salary is often cited as a key reason for recruiting challenges in the law enforcement community, and, indeed, insufficient salary was one of the most frequently mentioned downsides that recruits considered when contemplating a career in law enforcement. However, this survey corroborates past research in noting that many recruits are drawn to law enforcement for nonpecuniary reasons; further, the recruits surveyed in this study did not seem dissatisfied with the salary and benefits offered by the agency with which they accepted employment. Some important groups, including women, Asian recruits, and black recruits, tended to indicate that the salary offered by their agency was actually a factor that influenced their decision to accept the job offer.

These findings suggest that (1) law enforcement agencies should not assume that a low salary is a powerful deterrent to potential recruits and (2) greater emphasis on the nonfinancial benefits of law enforcement is warranted. In some labor markets, such as those in which suburban departments have salaries that are more than $10,000 higher than the major urban department, this may pose a problem. However, for other departments with which RAND has studied recruiting—the San Diego Police Department, for example (Ridgeway et al., 2008)—changes in recruiting practices alone, with no changes in base pay, have been able to increase applications and recruits. Law enforcement departments should not only show how their compensation and benefits compare favorably with other local employment options, as noted in the preceding recommendation, but should also highlight positive aspects of working in law enforcement, such as the prestige of the profession and its public service aspect. Calling candidates' attention to the nonpecuniary benefits of working in law enforcement may show how such a career can offer intrinsic rewards that may be just as important as, or more important than, external ones.

Fully Engage Current Officers and Staff in Agency Recruiting Efforts

As noted earlier, friends or family working at the department that recruits' ultimately joined were responsible for first prompting more than 40 percent of new recruits to consider the agency. An additional 20 percent were prompted by friends and family at another agency. In addition, half of the new recruits sought out the advice of law enforcement members when they were considering their career choices. These findings suggest that those expressly tasked with recruiting should not be the only agency employees working to attract promising candidates. On the contrary, a department's current officers and civilian staff can be among its most effective recruiters. In order to tap into this in-house resource, those directly responsible for recruiting may ask officers to accompany them to career fairs, for example, or develop other ways to connect prospective candidates directly with current law enforcement professionals. If necessary, the agency may develop training or guidance for employees who are interested in supporting recruitment in this manner yet could benefit from advice on how to make the most of such interactions (e.g., what aspects of law enforcement to emphasize, what types of questions to avoid posing to would-be recruits). When such interaction is less feasible, as may be the case for nonlocal would-be candidates, officers and staff could instead offer personal testimonials that can be used in recruiting materials (e.g., videos, public announcements). Moreover, agencies may consider offering incentives to current employees for successful referrals (e.g., a monetary bonus or extra vacation time for bringing in applicants who make it to a certain phase in the recruiting process). Simply publicizing hiring efforts and successes, including acknowledging the individuals responsible for new hires, may help promote the idea that recruiting is an agency-level effort to which all employees can contribute.

Expand the Agency's Internet Presence

When asked what first motivated them to contact their current employer, 18 percent of recruits surveyed cited an Internet ad. Other findings show that recruits use the Internet both often and broadly: 80 percent of respondents access the Internet at least daily, and large proportions of them use it for email, online information searches, online job searches, and social networking. While many large law enforcement departments have already invested resources to develop and maintain their own websites, there may be other, less costly ways that agencies can benefit from recruits', and, presumably, would-be recruits', extensive use of the Internet. Job listings could be posted on Internet job boards (e.g., CareerBuilder.com, Monster.com), advertisements could be designed to appear in response to information searches related to law enforcement, and an agency presence could be created on social networking sites such as Facebook and MySpace. Agencies could also work with local sources of prospective candidates, such as military installations, colleges, and universities, to send out mass emails regarding job opportunities to criminal justice majors and personnel separating from the military. These approaches may be relatively low-cost or even free, potentially enabling agencies to employ several of them. Such a multipronged Internet strategy may help make a specific law enforcement agency salient in the minds of prospective candidates, in addition to leaving them with a favorable impression of working in law enforcement.

Develop Strategies to Recruit a Workforce Well Suited to Community-Oriented Policing

At the outset of this report, we discussed how police officers and sheriff's deputies who vary in terms of their gender, race/ethnicity, immigrant status, and educational background may improve law enforcement departments' capacity to engage in community-oriented policing. Should law enforcement departments perceive a need to target certain types of recruits because of attrition, workforce growth, or a shift in hiring priorities, the results of our survey provide the means to do so. Specifically, law enforcement agencies can appeal to what different types of recruits view as advantages or benefits of working in law enforcement in conjunction with addressing what they perceive to be downsides of a law enforcement career.

For example, a department that is actively seeking to add more women to its ranks can customize a recruiting strategy specifically for women. In addition, profiling female leaders in the department can signal that women have opportunities to advance in the department, a key reason women cite for pursing law enforcement in the first place.

Along with women, Hispanic recruits were more likely to indicate that they entered law enforcement because of its opportunities for advancement. Asian recruits in particular valued the excitement of the work. Occupational prestige was a draw for several groups of interest, including black recruits, Hispanic recruits, and those from immigrant families, as was the public service aspect of the job. Stressing these different positive aspects of law enforcement, especially through outlets and in locations more likely to reach targeted groups of prospective candidates, may help departments attract more of the types of individuals they believe will complement the current workforce.

Turning our attention to perceived challenges or downsides of law enforcement, they also provide law enforcement agencies with opportunities to improve their recruiting. Understanding the barriers to entry is an important step toward developing a diverse force that is well positioned to engage in community-oriented policing in a diverse community. Equipped with information about what groups such as women or college graduates view as negative aspects of or barriers to law enforcement, agencies can develop strategies expressly intended to quell such misgivings. For example, college graduates were more inclined than less educated recruits to cite the negative portrayal of law enforcement in the media and perceived corruption in law enforcement departments as career field disadvantages. Agencies may address such concerns head-on by acknowledging past problems (if they exist) or correcting related misperceptions and by showing prospective recruits examples of positive portrayals by the media and other commendations for a job well done.

In a related vein, female recruits were more inclined than male recruits to report concerns about difficulties meeting fitness requirements. One way departments may alleviate this unease is to assess whether the fitness requirements, such as rescue drags and wall climbs, need to be tested during the recruiting process or whether certain skills can instead be acquired and practiced in the academy. Another approach may be to offer exercises classes or some sort of pre-academy "boot camp" that will prepare recruits to meet an agency's physical standards. In our survey, female recruits rated this potential strategy as more effective than did male recruits. In addition, it may be a useful way for prospective candidates to spend some of their time while waiting for their application to be processed or for training to commence. Some departments, such as the Los Angeles Police Department, provide new recruits with an exercise curriculum to get them prepared for the police academy. In a related example, the Sacramento Sheriff's Department developed a "Fitness Challenge" that it has credited with increasing the number of women entering its training academies. Many of the agency's female deputies are involved in this program, which entails dividing female candidates into teams. The teams then train together at a local fitness facility, and, at the end of 12 weeks, they compete and receive awards. Individual routines and training goals are also encouraged as part of the process (California Commission on POST, 2006).

Women also indicated that their peers felt they could not balance family obligations with a law enforcement career. Having a few female officers or deputies who have been able to balance family and career describe their experiences, either at recruiting events or on a recruiting website, might sway some women to reconsider.

Continue to Learn from New Recruits

This study demonstrates the value in not only surveying law enforcement professionals, as many past efforts have done, but also in focusing specifically on the newest additions to police and sheriff's departments. The results of this survey can serve not only as a source of ideas of recruiting strategies but also as a benchmark of sorts against which agencies may compare themselves over time. Will recruits' reasons for entering law enforcement change in the years to come? Will their views of law enforcement's disadvantages or the perceived usefulness of different recruitment strategies shift in light of economic changes or the law enforcement community's greater emphasis on community-oriented policing?

The survey instrument we utilized in this study, provided in Appendix A, can be used by law enforcement departments themselves to learn about different training academy cohorts. Administering the survey to multiple classes will enable agencies to study how recruits' perceptions of law enforcement in general and their employing agency in particular may evolve over time. In addition, questions from the survey could be adapted for use at an earlier point, during the recruitment and selection process, in order to learn about prospective candidates' reasons for pursuing a career in law enforcement, their key influencers, or other views. By continuing to "take the pulse" of new recruits in these ways, agencies can adjust their recruiting strategies as necessary to ensure the desired quantity *and* quality of applicants are obtained.

Survey Instrument

Background Information

The Office of Community Oriented Policing Services, U.S. Department of Justice has asked RAND's Center on Quality Policing to conduct a survey of recent police officer and sheriff deputy recruits from approximately 50 communities nationwide in order to help the law enforcement community improve its recruitment practices and results. RAND Corporation is a non-profit research institution headquartered in Santa Monica, CA that conducts independent, objective research and analysis to advance public policy. Information about RAND and its Center on Quality Policing is available at http://cqp.rand.org.

We are asking you to participate in this survey because you are a recent recruit in one of the law enforcement agencies included in our research. The survey consists primarily of multiple questions about your background, your opinions as a recent recruit, and your opinions about the recruiting of police officers and sheriff deputies more generally. It should take about 15 minutes to complete the survey.

This survey is completely voluntary. You do not have to participate, and you may choose to skip a specific question for any reason. However, we strongly encourage you to participate, as responses from your agency and others across the nation are necessary to ensure we have a representative sample upon which to provide the law enforcement community with concrete, actionable lessons for recruiting success.

We are not requesting any information that directly identifies you; we do not need your name, address, or other personal information. Your agency will *not* have access to your individual survey. Your survey will not be shared with anyone outside the RAND project team, and the hard copy of your survey will be destroyed after the study is complete.

The results of the survey will be featured on RAND's web site and in a published report. In addition, if enough of your fellow recruits complete the survey, your own agency will receive a customized survey report that features your agency's responses, as a group, and compares them with responses from other law enforcement agencies. Please note that findings from the survey will only be presented in summary form and will not be portrayed to identify a specific individual in any way.

If you have any questions about this survey, please feel free to write to RAND at COPS_survey@rand.org, and you will receive a response as soon as possible. You may also contact the lead researcher, Dr. Laura Castaneda, at 310-393-0411 x6897 or laurawc@rand.org.

To ensure your response can be included in our analysis, we request that you return your completed survey within **one month of receipt** using the self-addressed, stamped envelope that you were provided.

Thank you for sharing your time and insights in support of this study.

RAND Law Enforcement Officer Recruitment Survey

Background

This first section of the survey contains questions about your personal background, such as your gender, age, education, and military experience.

1. What is your gender?

   ❏ Male
   ❏ Female

2. In what year were you born?
   Year: 19 __

3. What is your marital status?

   ❏ Now married
   ❏ Widowed
   ❏ Divorced
   ❏ Separated
   ❏ Never married

4. How many children or legal dependents under the age of 18 do you have?

   __ children

5. Are you Spanish/Hispanic/Latino?

   ❏ No, not Spanish/Hispanic/Latino
   ❏ Yes, Mexican, Mexican American, Chicano
   ❏ Yes, Puerto Rican
   ❏ Yes, Cuban
   ❏ Yes, other Spanish/Hispanic/Latino

6. What is your race? Please mark (X) one or more races to indicate what you consider yourself to be.

☐ White
☐ Black or African American
☐ American Indian or Alaska Native
☐ Asian Indian
☐ Chinese
☐ Filipino
☐ Japanese
☐ Korean
☐ Vietnamese
☐ Other Asian
☐ Native Hawaiian
☐ Guamanian or Chamorro
☐ Samoan
☐ Other Pacific Islander
☐ Some other race (please specify): _____

7. Where were you born?

☐ In the United States—print name of state:

_____

☐ Outside the United States, but on U.S. territory (e.g., a U.S. military installation, Puerto Rico, Guam)
☐ Outside the United States—print name of foreign country.:

_____

8. How long have you and your family lived in the United States? Please select the statement that best reflects your family's experience in the United States.

☐ I was born in the United States, but both of my parents were born outside the United States.
☐ I was born in the United States, as was one of my parents. My other parent was born outside the United States.

❏ I was born in the United States, and both of my parents were also born in the United States, but not all of my grandparents were.

❏ My grandparents, my parents, and I were all born in the United States.

❏ Don't know

9. What is your current religious preference, if any? Please print the name of your religion in the space that follows or mark the box for "None."

_____

❏ None

10. What is the highest degree or level of school you have **completed**? Please mark (X) only **one** box. If currently enrolled, mark the previous grade or the highest degree received.

❏ High school graduate—high school diploma or equivalent (for example: GED) → Skip next question

❏ Some college credit, but less than 1 year

❏ 1 or more years of college, no degree

❏ Associate degree (for example: AA, AS)

❏ Bachelor's degree (for example: BA, AB, BS)

❏ Master's degree (for example: MA, MS, MEng, MEd, MSW, MBA)

❏ Professional degree (for example: MD, DDS, DVM, LLB, JD)

❏ Doctorate degree (for example: PhD, EdD)

11. If you attended college, what was your **most recent** field of study?

❏ Criminology, criminal justice, or law enforcement

❏ Pre-law or law school

❏ Math or engineering

❏ Business

❏ Natural or physical science

☐ Social science
☐ Pre-med, nursing, or other healthcare field
☐ Agriculture
☐ Liberal arts or humanities
☐ Other (please specify:) _____

12. Have you ever served on active duty in the U.S. Armed Forces, military Reserve, or National Guard?

    Active duty does not include training for the Reserve or National Guard, but **does** include activation, for example, for Operation Enduring Freedom or Operation Iraqi Freedom.

    ☐ Yes, on active duty during the last 12 months
    ☐ Yes, on active duty in the past, but not during the last 12 months
    ☐ No, training for the Reserve or National Guard only → **Skip to Question 14**
    ☐ No, never served in the military → **Skip to Question 16**

13. In total, how much active-duty military service have you had? Please enter the total number of time in the boxes that follow. If you served for less than one year in total, enter only months.

    __ years __ months

14. Are you currently in the Reserve or National Guard?

    ☐ Yes
    ☐ No

15. In which component or components have you served? Please mark (X) as many boxes that apply.

Active Components
❏ U.S. Army
❏ U.S. Air Force
❏ U.S. Marine Corps
❏ U.S. Navy
❏ U.S. Coast Guard

Reserve Components
❏ U.S. Army Reserve
❏ U.S. Air Force Reserve
❏ U.S. Marine Forces Reserve
❏ U.S. Navy Reserve
❏ U.S. Coast Guard Reserve
❏ U.S. Army National Guard
❏ U.S. Air National Guard

❏ Other, including foreign military service— print name of component or service:

_____

16. Immediately before you joined your current law enforcement agency, were you:

❏ A full time **student**?
❏ An **active duty member** of the Armed Forces?
❏ An employee of a **private for-profit** company or business, or of an individual, for wages, salary or commissions?
❏ An employee of a **private not-for-profit**, tax exempt, or charitable organization?
❏ A **local government** employee (city, county, etc.)?
❏ A **state government** employee?
❏ A **federal government** employee?
❏ Self-employed in **own not incorporated** business, professional practice or farm?
❏ Self-employed in **own incorporated** business, professional practice or farm?
❏ Working **without pay** in family business or farm?
❏ Unemployed but **looking for work**?
❏ Unemployed but **not looking for work**?

Your Career in Law Enforcement

This section of the survey contains questions about your decision to become a police officer or sheriff deputy, the law enforcement agency with which you are currently employed, and what influenced your decision to accept employment there.

17. Do you have previous experience working in law enforcement? Please mark (X) as many boxes that apply.

❑ Yes, for this law enforcement agency
❑ Yes, for another city or county law enforcement agency
❑ Yes, for a state law enforcement agency
❑ Yes, for a federal law enforcement agency
❑ Yes, in private sector law enforcement (e.g., private security company, security department for a private organization)
❑ Yes, while serving in the U.S. Armed Forces, military Reserve, or National Guard (e.g., military police, security forces)
❑ No
❑ Other (please specify:) _____

18. People give many reasons for why they became law enforcement officers. Below you will find some of the major reasons that law enforcement officers give. Using the scale that follows, please rate each reason for how large a part it played in **your** decision to pursue a career in law enforcement. **Circle the number** that best reflects your opinion about how important each reason was to you at the time of your decision.

Reasons	Unimportant		Somewhat Important		Very Important
Opportunities for advancement	1	2	3	4	5
Structured like the military (e.g., use of rank, command structure)	1	2	3	4	5
Good salary	1	2	3	4	5
Good retirement plan	1	2	3	4	5
Good health insurance benefits	1	2	3	4	5
The excitement of the work	1	2	3	4	5
It provides an opportunity to help people in the community	1	2	3	4	5
Job security	1	2	3	4	5
To fight crime	1	2	3	4	5
The prestige of the profession	1	2	3	4	5
You work on your own a lot; have a good deal of autonomy	1	2	3	4	5
The variety and non-routine nature of the work	1	2	3	4	5
To enforce laws of the society	1	2	3	4	5
Good camaraderie with your co-workers	1	2	3	4	5
The job carries power and authority	1	2	3	4	5
To gain experience for another job	1	2	3	4	5
There was a lack of other job alternatives	1	2	3	4	5
Other job alternatives were not as interesting	1	2	3	4	5

If you, your friends, and/or relatives were victims of crime, please rate the following two reasons as well. Otherwise, select "N/A" for not applicable.

Because I had friends or relatives who were victims of crime	1	2	3	4	5
	N/A (e.g., I do not have friends or relatives who were victims of crime)				
Because I was a victim of crime	1	2	3	4	5
	N/A (I was not a victim of crime)				

19. People sometimes obtain opinions from family members, friends, or professionals that influence their employment-related decisions. In the first column of the table that follows, you will find a list of people who could be a source of such opinions.

    In the second column, please indicate all the people who offered an opinion when you were deciding whether to work in law enforcement by marking (X) the corresponding box for each person.

    Only for the people who *did* offer an opinion (those for whom you marked a box), please answer the following questions:

    • "Does or did this person work in law enforcement?"
    • "How much did this person support your decision to work in law enforcement?

    If you did not seek advice from anyone, please select the last option, "No one."

Relation	This person offered an opinion when I was making my decision on whether to work in law enforcement	Does or did this person work in law enforcement?	How much did this person support your decision to work in law enforcement?				
			Strongly opposed	Opposed	Neutral	Favor	Strongly favor
Your biological father		Yes / No	1	2	3	4	5
Your step or adoptive father		Yes / No	1	2	3	4	5
Your biological mother		Yes / No	1	2	3	4	5
Your step or adoptive mother		Yes / No	1	2	3	4	5
Your brother or sister		Yes / No	1	2	3	4	5
Another relative		Yes / No	1	2	3	4	5
Your spouse or partner		Yes / No	1	2	3	4	5
Your girlfriend or boyfriend		Yes / No	1	2	3	4	5

Relation	This person offered an opinion when I was making my decision on whether to work in law enforcement	Does or did this person work in law enforcement?	How much did this person support your decision to work in law enforcement?				
			Strongly opposed	Opposed	Neutral	Favor	Strongly favor
Your friend—same generation		Yes No	1	2	3	4	5
Your friend—older generation (10+ years)		Yes No	1	2	3	4	5
Your co-worker		Yes No	1	2	3	4	5
Your professor, teacher, or counselor		Yes No	1	2	3	4	5
Someone with professional expertise in law enforcement		Yes No	1	2	3	4	5
A member of the clergy or other adult from your place of worship		Yes No	1	2	3	4	5
Other (Please describe):		Yes No	1	2	3	4	5
No one							

20. At how many law enforcement agencies did you apply for a position **in the last 12 months?**

___ agencies

21. Was your current law enforcement agency your first choice among those you considered?

❑ Yes
❑ No
❑ Don't know

22. On average, how long will (or does) the commute take from your primary residence to your law enforcement agency? Estimate your commute time to the agency's primary location or headquarters, not the training academy (if different).

___ minutes

23. What **first prompted you to consider** working as a police officer or sheriff deputy in your current law enforcement agency? In other words, what information sources and potential influences motivated you to contact your current employer? **Please mark (X) all that apply.**

❑ Newspaper ad
❑ Magazine/journal ad
❑ Radio ad
❑ Television ad
❑ Internet ad
❑ Billboard
❑ Posters
❑ Mass mailing
❑ Career fair
❑ Community organization
❑ High School outreach
   Explorer and/or Cadets program

❒ College outreach
❒ College Internships
❒ Military Installation (e.g., Transition Assistance Program) Open House at the Police Department
❒ Walk-in-Office
❒ Experience working with the agency in another capacity
❒ Referral from friend or family member not in law enforcement
❒ Referral from friend or family member who currently works or once worked in a **different** law enforcement agency
❒ Referral from friend or family member who currently works or once worked in the **same** law enforcement agency
❒ Other (please describe:) _____
❒ Don't know

24. Using the scale that follows, please indicate how much you agree or disagree that the following factors influenced your decision **to accept employment** at your current law enforcement agency.

	Strongly disagree	Disagree	Neither disagree nor agree	Agree	Strongly agree
Size of agency	1	2	3	4	5
First agency to offer me a position	1	2	3	4	5
Location of city or agency	1	2	3	4	5
Affordability of housing	1	2	3	4	5
Salary	1	2	3	4	5
Retirement plan	1	2	3	4	5
Health insurance benefits	1	2	3	4	5
Vacation time	1	2	3	4	5
Reputation of the agency	1	2	3	4	5
Friend or family member works or worked for this agency	1	2	3	4	5
Variety in assignments	1	2	3	4	5
Agency was willing to send me to academy	1	2	3	4	5
Time between initial application and entering academy	1	2	3	4	5
Cost of uniforms, gear, and supplies needed for academy	1	2	3	4	5
Work hours available to me, such as 10 or 12 hours shifts	1	2	3	4	5
I was already with the agency in another capacity	1	2	3	4	5
Other (Please describe:) _____	1	2	3	4	5

25. So far, you have been asked to discuss why you were interested in law enforcement in general and your current law enforcement agency in particular. When people make a decision about their employment, they often consider not only the "pros" or benefits but also the "cons" or disadvantages of that particular line of work. **When you were deciding** whether to pursue a career in law enforcement, what were the main "cons" or disadvantages that came to mind? **Please mark (X) those that apply to you.**

☐ Insufficient salary
☐ Insufficient health insurance benefits
☐ Long hours
☐ Shift work
☐ Personal health or medical limitations
☐ Difficulty meeting fitness requirements
☐ Difficulty meeting family obligations (e.g., child care, elder care)
☐ Threat of injury
☐ Threat of death
☐ Other career interests
☐ Family members' negative views regarding law enforcement
☐ Friends' negative views regarding law enforcement
☐ Negative portrayal of law enforcement in the media
☐ Military-like qualities such as use of rank and command structure
☐ Abuse of power or excessive force used by law enforcement officer(s)
☐ Perceived corruption within law enforcement agencies
☐ Perceived favoritism within law enforcement agencies
☐ Other reason (please specify:) _____

26. Think of **a good friend or a family member** who is close to you in age, but has opted not to pursue a career in law enforcement. **To the best of your knowledge**, which of the following reasons help explain why he or she has not pursued a law enforcement career? **Please mark (X) those that apply to the good friend or family member you are thinking about.**

☐ Insufficient salary
☐ Insufficient health insurance benefits
☐ Long hours
☐ Shift work
☐ His/her health or medical limitations
☐ Criminal record
☐ Difficulty meeting fitness requirements
☐ Difficulty meeting family obligations (e.g., child care, elder care)
☐ Threat of injury
☐ Threat of death
☐ Other career interests / already has a satisfying career
☐ Personal negative views regarding law enforcement
☐ Family members' negative views regarding law enforcement
☐ Friends' negative views regarding law enforcement
☐ Negative portrayal of law enforcement in the media
☐ Military-like qualities such as use of rank and command structure
☐ Abuse of power or excessive force used by law enforcement officer(s)
☐ Perceived corruption within law enforcement agencies
☐ Perceived favoritism within law enforcement agencies
☐ Other reason (please specify:) _____

27. To improve law enforcement recruiting, police officers and sheriff deputies have suggested the following actions or incentives. Using the scale that follows, please rate how effective you believe each action or incentive would be in helping to **improve recruiting in your current law enforcement agency.**

	Ineffective		Effective		Very effective
Better or more information about what the job actually entails	1	2	3	4	5
Better or more information about the community in which the agency is located	1	2	3	4	5
Higher starting salary	1	2	3	4	5
Signing bonus	1	2	3	4	5
Financial assistance for uniforms and other necessary supplies	1	2	3	4	5
Financial assistance for gym membership	1	2	3	4	5
Financial assistance to purchase a home (e.g., financing)	1	2	3	4	5
Financial assistance for job commute (e.g., public transportation voucher, mileage allowance)	1	2	3	4	5

	Ineffective		Effective		Very effective
Relocation assistance (e.g., information regarding community, housing search assistance, temporary housing)	1	2	3	4	5
Tuition assistance	1	2	3	4	5
Better pension or retirement benefits	1	2	3	4	5
Free training and exercise to help meet physical standards	1	2	3	4	5
Opportunities for professional development (e.g., management, investigations, technology)	1	2	3	4	5
Flexible work schedule	1	2	3	4	5
Choice in job duties or assignments	1	2	3	4	5
Child care during academy	1	2	3	4	5
Child care during regular employment	1	2	3	4	5
Better health insurance coverage	1	2	3	4	5
More vacation time	1	2	3	4	5
Opportunities for extended leave without pay	1	2	3	4	5
Other (please describe:) _____					

Volunteering and Other Non-Work Activities

The final section of the survey includes questions about how you typically spend your free time, to include volunteer work, hobbies, and Internet use.

28. **In the last year**, have you done any volunteer activities through or for an organization?

   ❒ Yes
   ❒ No → Skip to Question 31

29. How many different organizations have you **volunteered through or for in the last year**?

   ___ organizations

30. What type(s) of organization(s) are they? Mark (X) all that apply.

   ❒ Religious organization
   ❒ Children's educational, sports, or recreational group
   ❒ Other educational group
   ❒ Social and community service group
   ❒ Civic organization
   ❒ Cultural or arts organization
   ❒ Environmental or animal care organization
   ❒ Health research or health education organization
   ❒ Hospital, clinic, or healthcare organization
   ❒ Immigrant/refugee assistance
   ❒ International organization
   ❒ Labor union, business, or professional organization
   ❒ Political party or advocacy group
   ❒ Public safety organization
   ❒ Sports or hobby group
   ❒ Youth services organization
   ❒ Other (please describe:) _____

31. What types of activities do you regularly engage in during your free time? Mark (X) all that apply.

☐ Team sports
☐ Tennis
☐ Golf
☐ Hiking/camping
☐ Hunting/shooting
☐ Fishing
☐ Biking
☐ Jogging
☐ Swimming
☐ Martial arts
☐ Yoga
☐ Fitness classes or exercise at local gym
☐ Attending professional sporting events
☐ Attending concerts
☐ Attending movies in theatres
☐ Watching movies at home on DVDs
☐ Watching television
☐ Listening to the radio
☐ Playing video games
☐ Playing a musical instrument
☐ Reading
☐ Shopping
☐ Cooking
☐ Other (please describe:) _____

32. Which of the following ways have you used the Internet?

☐ E-mail
☐ Downloading music
☐ Downloading podcasts
☐ Gaming
☐ Online shopping
☐ Online job search

☐ Online information searches (e.g., driving directions, weather forecasts, directory assistance)
☐ News and current events sites
☐ Social networking sites (e.g., MySpace, Facebook)
☐ Other (please describe:) _____

33. **In the last year**, how many times have you accessed the Internet?

☐ Did not access within the past year
☐ Once or twice
☐ 3–5 times
☐ 6–11 times (less than monthly)
☐ Less than weekly (1–3 times month)
☐ Less than daily (1–3 times week)
☐ Almost daily (over 100 times)
☐ Daily or more (over 200 times)

34. Is there anything you would like the RAND research team to know about choosing a law enforcement career, your experience as a law enforcement officer recruit, or law enforcement officer recruiting in general? Please use the space below for any comments that you would like to share related to the topics covered in this survey or about the survey itself.

Thank you again for your time and input.

Please place your completed survey in the self-addressed, stamped envelope that you received and drop it in any U.S. Postal Service mailbox.

Description of Survey Responses

Table B.1a
Descriptive Statistics of Key Groups of Interest, Part 1

Characteristic	All	Sex		Race/Ethnicity			
		Men	Women	White	Asian	Black	Hispanic
N	1,619	1,332	282	846	46	296	388
Average age	27.8	27.7	28.7	27.4	30	29.6	27.7
Female (%)	16	0	100	13	19	28	17
Married (%)	29	30	26	32	24	25	25
Parents of children under 18 (%)	31	30	38	26	16	54	36
Asian (%)	3	3	3	0	100	0	0
Black (%)	14	12	24	0	0	100	0
Hispanic (%)	25	24	27	0	0	0	100
White (%)	56	58	45	100	0	0	0
Other (%)	3	3	2	0	0	0	0
Multiracial (%)	6	6	6	3	8	1	13
Immigrant family (%)	26	25	30	13	92	18	49
Bachelor's degree or higher (%)	41	39	51	46	37	37	32
Prior active duty military (%)	18	20	9	16	32	27	20
Currently serving in Guard or Reserve (%)	6	6	6	5	4	12	5
Prior law enforcement experience (%)	24	24	21	23	38	34	20

Table B.1b
Descriptive Statistics of Key Groups of Interest, Part 2

Characteristic	All	Age		Immigrant Family		College Graduate	
		25 and younger	26 and older	No	Yes	No	Yes
N	1,619	593	995	338	1,281	1,044	780
Average age	27.8	23.6	31.0	27.6	28.4	27.6	28.2
Female (%)	16	12	19	14	19	13	20
Married (%)	29	10	43	30	27	31	26
Parents of children under 18 (%)	31	9	47	32	29	36	25
Asian (%)	3	3	3	0	9	3	2
Black (%)	14	8	17	15	9	14	12
Hispanic (%)	25	20	28	17	47	29	19
White (%)	56	65	50	66	27	52	62
Other (%)	3	3	3	1	7	2	4
Multiracial (%)	6	7	5	6	6	6	5
Immigrant family (%)	26	18	32	0	53	23	30
Bachelor's degree or higher (%)	41	39	42	39	48	0	100
Prior active duty military (%)	18	11	25	20	15	24	12
Currently serving in Guard or Reserve (%)	6	5	6	6	5	6	7
Prior law enforcement experience (%)	24	21	25	24	23	26	20

Table B.1c
Descriptive Statistics of Key Groups of Interest, Part 3

Characteristic	All	Military Experience		Prior Law Enforcement Experience	
		No	Yes	No	Yes
N	1,619	1,250	369	1,173	446
Average age	27.8	27.4	29.7	27.5	29.0
Female (%)	16	18	8	17	14
Married (%)	29	26	40	27	35
Parents of children under age 18 (%)	31	26	54	29	41
Asian (%)	3	2	4	2	4
Black (%)	14	12	20	12	20
Hispanic (%)	25	24	26	26	21
White (%)	56	58	48	57	54
Other (%)	3	3	1	4	1
Multiracial (%)	6	6	7	6	6
Immigrant family (%)	26	27	21	30	25
Bachelor's degree or higher (%)	41	44	26	43	35
Prior active duty military (%)	18	0	100	16	28
Currently serving in Guard or Reserve (%)	6	0	31	5	8
Prior law enforcement experience (%)	24	21	35	0	100

Table B.2
Demographics of New Recruits: Age, Sex,
Family Status, and Religion

	Percentage, Average, or Range
Age (average)	27.3
Age (80% range)	22.5–30.5
Female	16%
Marital status	
Never married	65%
Now married	29%
Previously married	6%
Have children under 18	31%
Religion	
Non-Catholic Christian	31%
Catholic	36%
None	27%
Other	6%

Table B.3
Race, Ethnicity, and Heritage of New Recruits

	Percentage
Race/ethnicity (primary)	
Asian	3
Black	14
Hispanic	25
White	56
Other	3
Multiracial	6
Family immigration history	
All born in the United States	45
One or more grandparents are immigrants	19
One parent is an immigrant	8
Both parents are immigrants	12
Recruit is an immigrant	14
Do not know	2
Birthplace	
In the United States	86
Outside the United States	13
U.S. territory	1

Table B.4
Educational Attainment of New Recruits

	Percentage
Education	
High school graduate, or equivalent	11
Less than 1 year	7
More than 1 year, no degree	22
Associate degree	18
Bachelor's degree	38
Master's degree	3
Professional or doctoral degree	0
Field of study	
Criminology, criminal justice, or law enforcement	43
Liberal arts or humanities	16
Business	14
Social science	8
Math or engineering	6
Pre-med, nursing, or other health care field	6
Other	5
Natural or physical science	2
Pre-law or law school	1

Table B.5
Military Service of New Recruits

	Percentage or Average	
Military service		
Never served in military	79	
Reserve or National Guard training only	2	
Active duty in the past 12 months	7	
Active duty more than 12 months ago	12	
Years of service (average)	5.9 years	
Currently in Reserve/Guard	6	
Service component[a] (of those with military service)		**Relative composition of the U.S. military[b] (%)**
Active		
U.S. Marine Corps	29	13
U.S. Army	28	36
U.S. Navy	25	22
U.S. Air Force	11	21
U.S. Coast Guard	1	3
Reserve		
U.S. Army Reserve	14	12
U.S. Army National Guard	11	21
U.S. Navy Reserve	9	4
U.S. Marine Corps Reserve	7	2
U.S. Air Force Reserve	4	4
U.S. Air National Guard	4	6
U.S. Coast Guard Reserve	1	1

[a] Percentages under service branch add up to more than 100 percent because 34 percent of respondents reported serving in multiple branches.

[b] The relative composition of the military represents what we would expect if there was no relationship between service branch and being a new recruit.

Table B.6
Prior Employment of New Recruits

	Percentage
Prior employment	
For-profit	42
Local government	15
State government	2
Federal government	2
Active-duty military	4
Nonprofit	3
Student	26
Self-employed	3
Unemployed	6
Prior law enforcement experience	
This agency	5
Local government	7
State government	1
Federal government	1
Military police	4
Private	5
Other	2
None	76

Table B.7
Percentage Reporting the Importance of Various Reasons for Deciding
to Pursue a Career in Law Enforcement (1 = unimportant, 3 = somewhat
important, and 5 = very important)

Reason	1	2	3	4	5	N/A
Opportunities for advancement	1	3	14	27	51	4
Structured like the military	19	20	29	18	11	4
Good salary	3	6	28	29	31	3
Good retirement plan	1	1	10	25	60	4
Good health insurance benefits	1	1	12	28	54	3
The excitement of the work	1	3	12	28	52	4
It provides an opportunity to help people in the community	0	0	9	30	57	3
Job security	1	1	8	25	62	3
To fight crime	1	2	18	33	42	3
The prestige of the profession	2	6	21	32	35	4
You work on your own a lot; have a good deal of autonomy	7	17	28	30	15	3
The variety and nonroutine nature of the work	1	4	18	35	39	3
To enforce laws of the society	0	3	24	39	30	3
Good camaraderie with your co-workers	0	2	15	41	36	5
The job carries power and authority	13	20	31	21	12	3
To gain experience for another job	38	20	18	10	10	4
There was a lack of other job alternatives	55	17	14	7	4	4
Other job alternatives were not as interesting	27	12	26	19	12	3
Because I had friends or relatives who were victims of crime	13	7	11	10	7	51
Because I was a victim of crime	11	5	7	6	5	66

Table B.8
Number of Law Enforcement Agencies Applied to in the Past 12 Months

	Number of Agencies							
	0	1	2	3	4	5	6+	N/A
Percentage applying to that many agencies	18	41	19	12	5	2	1	3

Table B.9
Current Agency Was First Choice Among Those Considered

	Response			
	Yes	No	Don't Know	N/A
Percentage	77	19	3	2

Table B.10
Commute Time from Residence to Work (in minutes)

Average	40
80% range	15–90

Table B.11
Sources That First Prompted Recruits to Consider
Working as a Police Officer or Sheriff's Deputy in
Their Current Law Enforcement Agency

Source	Percentage
Newspaper ad	9
Magazine/journal ad	1
Radio ad	3
Television ad	5
Internet ad	18
Billboard	5
Posters	4
Mass mailing	1
Career fair	8
Community organization	1
High school outreach	1
Explorer and/or cadets program	3
College outreach	3
College internships	3
Military installation	3
Open house at police department	2
Walk-in-office	2
Experience working with the agency in another capacity	10
Referral from friend or family member not in law enforcement	12
Referral from friend or family member who works/worked in a different law enforcement agency	21
Referral from friend or family member who works/worked in the same law enforcement agency	41
Other	13
Don't know	6

Table B.12
Factors That Influenced Recruits' Decision to Accept Employment at Their Current Law Enforcement Agency (1 = strongly agree, 3 = neither agree nor disagree, 5 = strongly agree)

Factor	1	2	3	4	5	N/A
Retirement plan	1	1	14	37	47	0
Reputation of the agency	2	3	16	33	47	0
Health insurance benefits	1	2	13	39	45	0
Location of city or agency	4	4	22	31	38	0
Variety in assignments	2	4	23	36	35	0
Agency was willing to send me to academy	5	6	27	28	34	0
Size of agency	4	4	30	34	27	0
Friend or family member works or worked for this agency	19	8	27	22	24	0
Vacation time	3	8	32	35	22	0
Salary	4	10	25	41	20	0
First agency to offer me a position	15	14	30	24	17	0
Time between initial application and entering academy	10	12	43	19	16	0
Work hours available to me, such as 10- or 12-hour shifts	15	14	42	18	12	0
Affordability of housing	17	17	43	14	9	0
Cost of uniforms, gear, and supplies needed for academy	24	17	42	11	6	0
I was already with the agency in another capacity	43	15	32	5	5	0
Other	4	1	91	2	2	0

Table B.13
Percentage Reporting Having Done Any
Volunteer Activities Through or for an
Organization in the Past Year

	Response		
	Yes	No	N/A
Percentage	35	62	3

Table B.14
Number of Organizations That Recruits Report Having Done
Volunteer Activities Through or for in the Past Year

	Number of Organizations				
	1	2	3	4+	N/A
Percentage volunteering for that many organizations	48	32	12	3	5

Table B.15
Kinds of Organizations That Recruits Report Having Volunteered for in the Past Year

Organization Type	Percentage
Religious organization	10
Social and community service group	10
Children's educational, sports, or recreational group	9
Sports or hobby group	6
Youth services organization	4
Public safety organization	3
Hospital, clinic, or healthcare organization	3
Health research or health education organization	2
Civic organization	2
Cultural or arts organization	1
Environmental or animal care organization	1
International organization	1
Labor union, business, or professional organization	1
Political party or advocacy group	1
Immigrant/refugee assistance	0
Other educational group	2
Other	6

Table B.16
Types of Activities That Recruits Report Regularly Engaging in During Their Free Time

Activity	Percentage
Watching movies at home on DVDs	65
Watching television	63
Attending movies in theaters	57
Jogging	46
Fitness classes or exercise at local gym	44
Listening to the radio	43
Team sports	37
Attending professional sporting events	34
Playing video games	34
Reading	34
Cooking	30
Shopping	25
Attending concerts	22
Fishing	18
Hiking/camping	17
Swimming	17
Biking	15
Hunting/shooting	15
Golf	13
Playing a musical instrument	10
Martial arts	9
Tennis	5
Yoga	5
Other	12

References

Baker, Al, and Steven Greenhouse, "Arbitration Panel Gives Raise to City Police Officers," *New York Times*, May 20, 2008.

California Commission on Peace Officer Standards and Training, *Recruitment and Retention Best Practices Update*, 2006. As of January 19, 2010: http://www.post.ca.gov/training/bestpractices/bestpractices-recruitment.asp

Castro, Hector, "Bad Economy Good for Police Recruiting: From Bust to Boom in a Short Time," *Seattle Post-Intelligencer*, October 2, 2009.

Dardick, Hal, and Angela Rozas, "Top Cop Gets Lesson in Chicago Politics from City Council," *Chicago Tribune*, July 16, 2008.

Guillen, Joe, "Cleveland Sends Layoff Notices to Safety Forces," *Cleveland Plain Dealer*, December 23, 2009.

Hageman, M. J. C., "Who Join the Police for What Reasons: An Argument for the 'New Breed,'" *Journal of Police Science Administration*, Vol. 7, No. 2, 1979, pp. 206–210.

LaTourrette, Tom, David S. Loughran, and Seth A. Seabury, *Occupational Safety and Health for Public Safety Employees: Assessing the Evidence and the Implications for Public Policy*, Santa Monica, Calif.: RAND Corporation: MG-792-CHSWC/NIOSH, 2008. As of July 15, 2010: http://www.rand.org/pubs/monographs/MG792/

Lester, David, "Why Do People Become Police Officers: A Study of Reasons and Their Predictions of Success," *Journal of Police Science and Administration*, Vol. 11, No. 2, 1983, pp. 170–174.

Lim, Nelson, Carl Matthies, Greg Ridgeway, and Brian Gifford, *To Protect and to Serve: Enhancing the Efficiency of LAPD Recruiting*, Santa Monica, Calif.: RAND Corporation, MG-881-RMPF, 2009. As of July 15, 2010: http://www.rand.org/pubs/monographs/MG881/

Lonsway, Kim, Margaret Moore, Penny Harrington, Eleanor Smeal, and Katherine Spillar, *Hiring and Retaining More Women: The Advantages to Law Enforcement Agencies*, Beverly Hills, Calif.: National Center for Women and Policing, Spring 2003. As of July 15, 2010:
http://www.womenandpolicing.org/pdf/NewAdvantagesReport.pdf

Meagher, M. S., and N. A. Yentes, "Choosing a Career in Policing: A Comparison of Male and Female Perceptions," *Journal of Police Science Administration*, Vol. 14, No. 4, 1986, pp. 320–327.

National Public Safety Information Bureau, National Directory of Law Enforcement Administrators, 2008. As of July 21, 2010:
http://www.safetysource.com/

Orvis, Bruce R., Narayan Sastry, and Laurie L. McDonald, *Military Recruiting Outlook: Recent Trends in Enlistment Propensity and Conversion of Potential Enlisted Supply*, Santa Monica, Calif.: RAND Corporation, MR-677-A/OSD, 1996. As of July 15, 2010:
http://www.rand.org/pubs/monograph_reports/MR677/

Police Recruiting and Retention Clearinghouse, website, 2010. As of July 15, 2010:
http://www.rand.org/ise/centers/quality_policing/cops/

Raganella, Anthony J., and Michael D. White, "Race, Gender, and Motivation for Becoming a Police Officer: Implications for Building a Representative Police Department," *Journal of Criminal Justice*, Vol. 32, 2004, pp. 501–513.

Raymond, Barbara, Laura J. Hickman, Laura L. Miller, and Jennifer S. Wong, *Police Personnel Challenges After September 11: Anticipating Expanded Duties and a Changing Labor Pool*, Santa Monica, Calif.: RAND Corporation, OP-154-RC, 2005. As of July 15, 2010:
http://www.rand.org/pubs/occasional_papers/OP154/

Reaves, Brian A., and Matthew J. Hickman, *Law Enforcement Management and Administrative Statistics, 2000: Data for Individual State and Local Agencies with 100 or More Officers*, Washington, D.C.: Bureau of Justice Statistics, NCJ 203350, March 2004.

Reston, Maeve, and Phil Willon, "L.A. Councilman Considers Police, Firefighter Layoffs," *Los Angeles Times*, February 2, 2010.

Ridgeway, Greg, Nelson Lim, Brian Gifford, Christopher Koper, Carl Matthies, Sara Hajiamiri, and Alexis Huynh, *Strategies for Improving Officer Recruitment in the San Diego Police Department*, Santa Monica, Calif.: RAND Corporation, MG-724-SDPD, 2008. As of July 15, 2010:
http://www.rand.org/pubs/monographs/MG724/

Rostker, Bernard D., William M. Hix, and Jeremy M. Wilson, *Recruitment and Retention: Lessons for the New Orleans Police Department*, Santa Monica, Calif.: RAND Corporation, MG-585-RC, 2007. As of July 15, 2010:
http://www.rand.org/pubs/monographs/MG585/

Ryan, Ann M., S. David Kriska, Bradley J. West, and Joshua M. Sacco, "Anticipated Work/Family Conflict and Family Member Views: Role in Police Recruiting," *Policing: An International Journal of Police Strategies & Management*, Vol. 24, 2001, pp. 228–239.

San Diego Police Department and Buck Consultants, *The City of San Diego Police Classification Compensation and Benefits Survey Results*, San Diego, Calif.: San Diego Police Department, 2006.

Scrivner, Ellen, *Innovations in Police Recruitment and Hiring: Hiring in the Spirit of Service*, Washington, D.C.: U.S. Department of Justice, Office of Community Oriented Policing Services, 2006. As of July 15, 2010: http://www.cops.usdoj.gov/files/ric/Publications/innovationpolicerecruitmenthiring.pdf

Seklecki, Richard, and Rebecca Paynich, "A National Survey of Female Police Officers: An Overview of Findings," *Police Practice and Research*, Vol. 8, No. 1, 2007, pp. 17–30.

Slater, Harold P., and Martin Reiser, "A Comparative Study of Factors Influencing Police Recruitment," *Journal of Police Science and Administration*, Vol. 16, 1988, pp. 168–176.

Taylor, Bruce, Bruce Kubu, Lorie Fridell, Carter Rees, Tom Jordan, and Jason Cheney, *The Cop Crunch: Identifying Strategies for Dealing with the Recruiting and Hiring Crisis in Law Enforcement*, Washington, D.C.: Police Executive Research Forum, December 30, 2005. As of July 15, 2010: http://www.ncjrs.gov/pdffiles1/nij/grants/213800.pdf

U.S. Department of Justice, Bureau of Justice Statistics, Law Enforcement Management and Administrative Statistics (LEMAS): 2003 Sample Survey of Law Enforcement Agencies [Computer file]. ICPSR04411-v1. Ann Arbor, Mich.: Inter-University Consortium for Political and Social Research [producer and distributor], 2006.

U.S. Department of Labor, Bureau of Labor Statistics, "Census of Fatal Occupational Injuries, 2008," 2009. As of July 15, 2010: http://www.bls.gov/iif/oshwc/cfoi/cfoi_rates_2008hb.pdf

Whetstone, Thomas S., John C. Reed, Jr., and Phillip C. Turner, "A Comparative Study of the Recruiting Practices of State Police Agencies," *International Journal of Police Science and Management*, Vol. 8, 2006, pp. 52–66.

Wilson, Jeremy M., and Clifford A. Grammich, *Police Recruitment and Retention in the Contemporary Urban Environment: A National Discussion of Personnel Experiences and Promising Practices from the Front Lines*, Santa Monica, Calif.: RAND Corporation, CF-261-DOJ, 2009. As of July 15, 2010: http://www.rand.org/pubs/conf_proceedings/CF261/

Yim, Youngyol, "Girls, Why Do You Want to Become Police Officers? Career Goals/Choices Among Criminal Justice Undergraduates," *Women & Criminal Justice*, Vol. 19, 2009, pp. 120–136.